In Jesus' Strong Hands

In Jesus' Strong Hands

Victors Instead of Victims

(Acts 17—28)

by

Randal Earl Denny

Wipf & Stock
PUBLISHERS
Eugene, Oregon

Wipf and Stock Publishers
199 W 8th Ave, Suite 3
Eugene, OR 97401

In Jesus' Strong Hands
Victors Instead of Victims (Acts 17-28)
By Denny, Randal E.

ISBN: 1-59244-957-3
Publication date 10/18/2004
Previously published by Beacon Hill Press, 1989

KJV—King James Version.

10 9 8 7 6 5 4 3 2 1

To

The Master's Men,
harmonious in heart and song,
a dream come true

Contents

Preface

A woman had been diagnosed as having cancer. While spending many hours undergoing medical tests, her husband paced the floor of the waiting room and drank coffee in the cafeteria for a change of view. After skimming all the available magazines without comprehending, he tiptoed into the hospital's chapel.

Under the veneer of manhood, he choked back his tears. Right when the pressures seemed too much to bear, he felt a strong hand on his shoulder. Somehow he sensed it was the chaplain. Suddenly he cried from deep down inside. His body shook with sobs. The chaplain stood by him, his strong hand somehow imparting the touch of tender strength. That strong hand of comfort eloquently released courage in the husband's heart. He could go on and face the unknown.

In Acts 17 through 28, Paul passes through tough times, through the unexpected, through testings and storms. Yet, through it all, Paul finds himself "in Jesus' strong hands." Jesus imparts courage to face life as it comes.

Dr. Lloyd Ogilvie told of having lunch with a market research analyst who polls what people think and how they feel. He said to Dr. Ogilvie, pastor of a large congregation: "Don't forget the needs of people. They are living with tremendous stress and they need courage. Just know this: when you help them to live courageously, you will always be on target."[1]

Luke's graphic descriptions and portrayals of events are right "on target." He enables us to see that we, too, are kept "in Jesus' strong hands."

Walter B. Knight exclaimed, "We do not know what the future holds, but we know the One who holds the future, the One in whose pierced hands reposes all power in heaven and on earth." In all life's circumstances, we may rest "in Jesus' strong hands"!

Acknowledgments

I've noticed how cooks enjoy preparing delicious dishes for people who are hungry and appreciative. In the same way, I enjoy preparing messages from God's Word for receptive and appreciative people—Spokane Valley Church of the Nazarene in particular. I owe a great debt to my "encouragers," who have chosen to be victors instead of victims. They help bring me along!

Appreciation is hereby expressed for permission to quote from copyrighted material as follows:

Beacon Hill Press of Kansas City: George and Donna Rench, *Spice and Rice.*

Fleming H. Revell Company: William P. Barker, *They Stood Boldly.*

Nazarene Publishing House: John Oster, "Our Island of Need," *Christ for the Nations;* William A. Tolbert, *Herald of Holiness,* Aug. 1, 1978.

Zondervan Publishing House: M. R. DeHaan, *Pentecost and After.*

I owe a great debt to my wife, Ruth, who encourages me to keep writing even when I lose sight of its ministry to others. People who surround me day after day give me inspiration and motivation to continue the adventure into God's Word and to enjoy the zest of the hunt!

1

Good Views Versus Good News

Acts 17

Billy Graham announced: "I intend to go anywhere, sponsored by anybody, to preach the gospel of Christ, *if there are no strings attached to my message.*"

That's Paul's attitude upon his release from the Philippian jail. Passing through several Greek towns, the evangelistic team arrived in Thessalonica. As often in the past, Paul and his men—in the power of the Holy Spirit—produced a revival and a riot. Looking for the missionary band, a mob shouted, "These that have turned the world upside down are come hither also" (v. 6, KJV). Christians turn their world upside down in order to make it right side up!

Moving on to the next stop, Paul and Silas arrived in Berea. As Paul preached the good news of Jesus, "Many of the Jews believed, as did also a number of prominent Greek women and many Greek men" (v. 12). However, angry Jews from Thessalonica heard about Paul's ministry in Berea and came stirring up trouble. Paul left alone, with Silas and Timothy remaining to strengthen the new church in Berea.

The lone missionary arrived in Athens, cultural center of the world, around A.D. 52. The sun of Athens' splendor and power had set long ago. Corinth had become the main Greek city, and Rome was now the political capital of the world. Everywhere Paul looked, he saw signs and symbols of a departed glory.

"While Paul was waiting for them in Athens, he was greatly distressed to see that the city was full of idols" (v. 16). In Paul's time, more than 30,000 public statues filled Athens, and many more graced private homes. In Athens, religion dealt with art and amusement, leaving the people morally destitute.

On the Acropolis, Paul saw the finest statuary in the world. Pace-setting architecture abounded; the Parthenon was a masterpiece without mortar. As Charles Ludwig pointed out, "Yet even with these skills, the Greeks were unhappy. Across the centuries they had learned that the sharpest chisels could not repair a broken heart."[1]

Though tourists through the ages beheld great beauty, Paul "was greatly distressed" because he knew empty-hearted people had bowed down to worship things made by their own hands. Unable to contain himself, Paul spoke to three different groups.

First, Paul spoke in the synagogue: "So he reasoned in the synagogue with the Jews and the God-fearing Greeks" (v. 17). These people were the ineffective religious, isolating themselves and their religion from the mainstream of society and life. They could not deliver their city from spiritual darkness because they focused too much on themselves.

Second, Paul spoke in the marketplace: "So he reasoned . . . in the marketplace day by day with those who happened to be there" (v. 17). These people were the naively religious, following along unthinkingly with whatever gods were in vogue at the time. Common workmen and merchants, citizens and slaves were unthinking victims of idolatry. Ray Stedman observed, "They were sunken in superstition and gripped by fear, uncertainty, dread of darkness, and inner tensions and turmoil—all results of following false gods."[2]

Third, Paul spoke on the Areopagus (Mars' Hill): "Paul then stood up in the meeting of the Areopagus and said: 'Men of Athens! I see that in every way you are very religious'" (v. 22). These people were the philosophers, the irreligious. Near the Acropolis, Mars' Hill was the place where one of the most powerful courts of justice met. Attempting to be fair and just, they guarded against human emotion. It was unlawful to make an emotional appeal. In fact, trials were held at night so that judges could not be unduly affected by facial expressions of defendants or witnesses. Reason and philosophy were their alternatives to the gods.

Athenians were caught up in the search for some satisfying good views about life and its ultimate meaning. What they really needed was good news about God's grace and mercy. As Paul confronted them, it is "good views" versus "good news."

Paul's Audience Rummaged for "Good Views"

In looking for a good view of life, Athens consorted with many gods. Early in time man began asking, "Who am I? Why am I here?" Becoming aware of the mysteries of nature, man became fearful and puzzled. Man needed protection from enemies, wild beasts, lightning, volcanoes, and earthquakes. He needed explanations. So he created divinities of his own image, ascribing to them power over nature that he didn't have.

By honoring the gods with temples and sacrifices, he could call upon them to take away his fears and dangers, to help him reach his goals. It was often said in Athens, "It's easier to find an idol than to find a man." Roy Smith noted, "The Greeks had many gods. In fact their Parthenon was packed with divinities, big and little, but still there was something lacking. Underneath all their learning, culture . . . and religious liberality, there was an instinctive feeling that they had not yet found the spiritual secret of the universe."[3]

In our day we stuff our houses with piles of materialism, attempting to salve the aching emptiness of spirit. A recent bumper sticker said, "The one with the biggest pile of toys wins!" We erect altars of shallow loyalties and conditional commitments, but the heart of mankind still seeks some satisfying answer.

In looking for a good view of life, Athens conceived an unknown god. With life's meaning so uncertain, they took no chances. Having built altars to every conceivable god, they reached out in a last desperate effort to find reality and erected altars "to an Unknown God." They wanted to be sure, just in case they had forgotten a god.

Ancient Romans, frightened by an earthquake or some cataclysmic event, would cry out to an unknown god. Today we say we believe this or that, but to whom do we cry out when frightened to death? We wonder if we have all the bases covered. God made us in such a way that we cannot rest until we have found the adequate person of Jesus to build our faith around. Our poor old world is in crisis, searching for meaning to life. People are skeptical but are yearning for a belief in something or someone that will satisfy.

In Tennessee Williams' play *The Night of the Iguana,* Hannah says to the backslidden preacher: "Liquor isn't your problem, Mr. Shannon."

He asks, "What is my problem?"

She replies, "The oldest one in the world—the need to believe in something or in someone—almost anyone—almost anything—something."

That's the problem of the Athenians and people today!

One writer observed, "In the play, *Man of La Mancha,* . . . Cervantes is accused of being a poet, an idealist, and of turning his back on life. His accuser ends with the words, 'A man must come to terms with life as it is.'

"To which Cervantes replies, 'I am 50 years old, and I have seen life as it is. I have been a soldier and have watched my comrades fall in battle. I have looked into their eyes during their last moments, eyes that asked the question, "why?" I do not believe they were asking why they were dying but rather why they had lived?'"[4]

Altars to an unknown god show inner desperation and uncertainty in the search for life's meaning.

In looking for a good view of life, Athens considered no gods. Four groups of philosophers gathered in Athens. Plato had founded the Academics. Aristotle originated the Peripatetics school. The other two groups, Epicureans and Stoics, got locked into discussion with Paul. These were the prevailing schools at the dawn of the Christian era. Neither believed in the resurrection of the body, so Paul's message of Jesus and the Resurrection caused quite a stir. It didn't fit their good views of life.

Epicurus founded his sect around 340 B.C. in Athens, his birthplace. He taught that pleasure—gratification of the senses—is the key to life. Like many modern Americans today, Epicureans were practical atheists. Oh, yes, they believed in the gods, but in name only. To them the gods made no practical difference in everyday life. The gods were too far away to be of much concern; therefore sacrifices and prayer mean nothing.

Since, for all practical purposes, the gods don't exist, they claimed, no moral law is written in the heart. Human laws are simply popularly conceived traditions, subject to whimsical change. New moralities change with new "good views." Each person decides his own idea of what pleases him; so, most people settle for a life of ease and self-indulgence. Today's Epicurean motto says, "Do your own thing!"

This good view of life portrays man as nonrational, a creature of emotion. Therefore, pleasure is the chief good; pain is the chief evil. Materialism remains in vogue, since this life is the only one that counts. We might as well get the most out of it. "Eat, drink and be merry, for tomorrow we die!" (1

Cor. 15:32, Phillips). Epicureans are existentialists—life is for just this moment. Pagan America has embraced that view of life, hook, line, and sinker!

The other good view is also contemporary: Stoicism. Zeno, the founder, was born about 30 B.C. on the island of Cyprus, Barnabas' birthplace. Coming to Athens, Zeno gathered his followers on a certain porch on the Acropolis. The Greek word for porch is *stoa,* and it gave rise to the name, Stoics. Zeno committed suicide, and self-destruction became common among his followers because his teachings led to a deep sense of futility.

Stoics did not deny the existence of the gods, but they believed life was governed by blind fate. Their concept of God was pantheistic: God is in everything everywhere. He exists in rocks and trees and flowers and animals and humans and mushrooms. Life after death, for them, meant some kind of impersonal continuance in the stream of reality—more rocks, trees, flowers, people, and mushrooms.

Ignoring emotions, Stoics taught that man is a rational being. He can have peace of mind only by being reasonable. Man must handle his own affairs by true wisdom and mastery over circumstances. One should never shrink from circumstances beyond control but maintain calm acceptance. Stoics prided themselves in being able to take whatever fate might throw at them. Their motto today urges, "Grin and bear it!"

Apathy is the chief virtue—unruffled apathy, indifference to pain or pleasure. One should never get overemotional about tragedy or happiness. In their efforts to remain detached and unemotional, Stoics shut out sympathy for others.

Stoics today can pass by tragedy unmoved and unsympathetic because they don't want to get involved. Human suffering makes them neither concerned nor mad. America has adopted their proud pagan fatalism: "Whatever will be, will be." And that can even be masked in theology under "the sovereignty of God."

For Stoics, universal law is supreme, and they must measure up and reach ethical perfection. Like the Pharisees who dogged Jesus' steps, they found ethical perfection impossible but pretended they had it. Thus they deeply resent the idea of needing forgiveness and reconciliation with God. A recent popular song spouts the same Stoic paganism: "I Did It My Way."

To such an audience, Paul had the audacity to preach Jesus and the Resurrection: "For the message of the cross is foolishness to those who are perishing, but to us who are being saved it is the power of God. For it is written: 'I will destroy the wisdom of the wise; the intelligence of the intelligent I will frustrate.' Where is the wise man? Where is the scholar? Where is the philosopher of this age? Has not God made foolish the wisdom of the world? . . . God was pleased through the foolishness of what was preached to save those who believe. Jews demand miraculous signs and Greeks look for wisdom, but we preach Christ crucified" (1 Cor. 1:18-23).

Athenians began to argue with Paul: "Some of them asked, 'What is this babbler trying to say?' Others remarked, 'He seems to be advocating foreign gods.' They say this because Paul was preaching the good news about Jesus and the resurrection" (v. 18). Greeks had personified other virtues such as Shame, Reason, Hatred, and Love and made gods out of them. As Paul preached "Jesus and the Resurrection," they thought he meant "Jesus and *Anastasis,*" the Greek word for "resurrection." They assumed that Paul was advocating the name of a new goddess, Anastasis, to be worshiped along with Jesus: "He seems to be advocating foreign gods" (in the plural). They complained, "Oh, no—not another 'Good View'!"

Paul's Audience Required the "Good News"

Paul had no idea of presenting Christianity as an alternate view. He knew they desperately needed the good news about Jesus. Christ is the only adequate answer for the spirit of man.

The Good News begins where you are. Paul introduced his sermon on Mars' Hill: "Men of Athens! I see that in every way you are very religious. For as I walked around and looked carefully at your objects of worship, I even found an altar with this inscription: TO AN UNKNOWN GOD. Now what you worship as something unknown I am going to proclaim to you" (vv. 22-23).

Yes, Greeks were religious; in fact, Athenian Greeks were unusually open to the good news of Jesus Christ. Without knowing why, they were hungry for Christ. Greek philosophies had been a schoolmaster bringing the Greek mind to the need for Christ. Much as the Old Testament law had been the "schoolmaster" leading Jews to the message of God's grace (Gal. 3:24, KJV), so the futility of human goodness prepared Greeks for the Good News. The gospel begins right where we are:

Just as I am, without one plea
But that Thy blood was shed for me.
—Charlotte Elliott

With a stroke of genius, Paul didn't attack their religions but used their "Unknown God" as a tool of evangelism. Christianity had not received legal status yet, but worship of the "Unknown God" was legal. Paul wisely capitalized on it: "You are right. There is One you don't know. He does exist. You can't reach Him with your rituals. But He is the One you must know. Let me tell you about Him!"

Six hundred years before Paul came to Athens, a terrible plague blighted the city. Nothing seemed to stop it. Epimenides, a poet, suggested a plan. A flock of sheep was turned loose to roam the city of Athens. Wherever a sheep lay down, it was sacrificed to the nearest god. If a sheep lay down where there was no god, it was sacrificed to "An Unknown God."

That's why Athens had so many shrines to "An Unknown God."

Paul knew firsthand of one complete and sufficient Sacrifice: "the Lamb of God, who takes away the sin of the world!" (John 1:29). His sermon zeroed in on the idea that though God is unknown, He is knowable!

The Good News explains who God is. Paul began with natural theology and moved toward revealed theology. His sermon had three main lines of thought.

First, God is Lord of all: "The God who made the world and everything in it is the Lord of heaven and earth and does not live in temples built by hands" (v. 24). Paul simply started where the Bible begins: "In the beginning God created the heavens and the earth" (Gen. 1:1). God is revealed in creation —if you'll take the time and diligence to study it. God is revealed in the march of history. His plan unfolds according to His time schedule and progress sheet. You can see it if you'll study with an unbiased mind.

Paul added this quotation: "For in him we live and move and have our being" (v. 28). The first verb, "we live," points to our physical life. The second verb, "we . . . move," or better, "we are moved," refers to the passions that move us: fear, love, hate, and so on. That points to our soul or emotional life. The third verb, "we . . . have our being," points to our spirit including our volitional life. We can't get away from God. We are totally dependent upon Him.

God is not created but is the Creator!

Second, God is Creator of all: "From one man he made every nation of men, that they should inhabit the whole earth . . . we are God's offspring" (vv. 26, 29). He made us all. He loves each one of us. Jews had divided their world into Jews and Gentiles. Greeks had divided theirs into Greeks and barbarians. Romans had divided theirs into citizens and conquered. But God made us all. He wants to be Father to all of us.

Paul says of God the Father, "He is not served by human hands, as if he needed anything" (v. 25). God may not need us, but does He want us?

One preacher took a handful of flowers into the pulpit and said, "These flowers were gathered for me by little hands. . . . Did I need them? No. Did I want them? (Of course!) . . . Your little girl kissed you before you left . . . this morning. Did you need it? . . . Did you want it?"[5]

We are decidedly wanted by God. He is "not willing that any should perish" (2 Pet. 3:9, KJV). God has done everything possible without violating our free will in order to woo us to himself: "For God so loved the world that he gave his one and only Son, that whoever believes in him shall not perish but have eternal life" (John 3:16).

Third, God is available to all: "God did this so that men would seek him and perhaps reach out for him and find him, though he is not far from each one of us" (v. 27). Paul spoke about "reaching out" for God. He used a word describing a person groping, feeling his way in the dark or being blindfolded.

Helen Keller, when told about God, replied that she knew Him already, *groping in the dark* after Him. The Bible says: "'You will . . . find me when you seek me with all your heart. I will be found by you,' declares the Lord" (Jer. 29: 13-14). God is reachable, and He is reaching out for you and me. Paul said, "He is not far from each one of us" (v. 27).

On March 2, 1791, John Wesley went home to be with the Lord at the age of 88. He had preached the Good News for 53 years. Before he died, he told his friends standing near, "The best of all is, God is with us." And again, lifting his hand, he repeated the same victorious words, "The best of all is, God is with us!"

The Good News is that we meet God through repentance: "In the past God overlooked such ignorance, but now he commands all people everywhere to repent" (v. 30). On

Mars' Hill, Paul cried for repentance. It wasn't a popular subject then, and it isn't now. John the Baptist preached repentance and was beheaded. Jesus preached repentance and was crucified. Peter preached repentance and was imprisoned. Paul preached repentance everywhere and was beheaded outside Rome. Yet repentance is the only attitude by which we receive God's forgiveness. The Bible teaches repentance, commands repentance, and urges repentance.

Our modern society offers four solutions to man's hopeless state:

"The first says, 'Learn.' Education is the answer. But education without God only makes a more dangerous [sinner]. There are enough Ph.D.'s in the average state penitentiary to staff a good-sized college. . . .

"The second says, 'Earn.' Our salvation is in economic progress. It is argued that if we can but salve the sores of poverty and distress that gnaw away at the hearts of our cities, we shall find the cure for society's ills.

"The third says, 'Burn.' Society, some argue, is so rotten that the only answer is to destroy it. But destroy it for what? To raise another like it on the ashes? . . . an exercise in futility.

"The fourth echoes an ancient source with a modern meaning. The word of God . . . is 'Turn.'"[6]

Repentance is turning to God. Repentance is recognizing and turning from our sins and confessing them to God. Repentance is a turning around, a change, a new life direction. A little girl explained repentance as "being sorry enough to say so, and then to quit doing it!"

A repentant person is willing to say, "Lord, I'm sorry. I recognize my sin. I confess it to You." We must not attempt to explain or excuse our sins. We must turn to God for His gracious forgiveness and help.

According to Paul's sermon on Mars' Hill, three facts call us to repentance.

First, there's the fact of an inescapable day of judgment: "For he has set a day when he will judge the world with justice by the man he has appointed" (v. 31). There is a great day coming when your life and mine shall be opened before God, and we shall hear God's decisive judgment!

Second, there's the fact of an inevitable Judge of all. He cannot be bribed, bought off, or persuaded. The Bible says, "This will take place on the day when God will judge men's secrets through Jesus Christ, as my gospel declares" (Rom. 2:16).

Third, there's the fact of an indisputable resurrection of Jesus: "He has given proof of this to all men by raising him from the dead" (v. 31). The resurrection of Jesus is God's dynamic proof of eternal life.

At Red Square in Moscow, Lenin's embalmed body lies in state. On his casket it says: "He was the greatest leader of all peoples, of all countries, of all times. He was the lord of the new humanity. He was the savior of the world."

But the eloquence of that description is all in the past tense. How unlike the triumphant, forward-looking words of Jesus: "I am the Living One . . . I am alive for ever and ever!" (Rev. 1:18). That's the victorious basis for our Good News.

Paul's Audience Reacted to "Good Views" Versus "Good News"

What happened when good news confronted good views? "When they heard about the resurrection of the dead, some of them sneered, but others said, 'We want to hear you again on this subject.' . . . A few men became followers of Paul and believed. Among them was Dionysius, a member of the Areopagus, also a woman named Damaris, and a number of others" (vv. 32, 34). Their reactions were typical of our day.

Some reacted with derision: They mocked. About all you can do for a mocker is to pray for him.

The outspoken agnostic Robert Ingersoll wrote a book in the 1800s titled *Some Mistakes of Moses.* He said in his book, "In 25 years . . . the Bible will be a forgotten book."

Dr. George Sweeting said, "Out of curiosity, I went to Chicago's Randolph Street Library and checked out his book. I was the first to do so in 20 years. Then I called the large Kroch's and Brentano's bookstore and asked for *Some Mistakes of Moses.* 'We don't have it,' the clerk informed me. Nor could she get it.

"'Do you have Bibles?' I asked.

"'Oh, yes. How many would you like?'

"'I really don't need any, but wondered how they were selling,' I responded. I learned that the Bible is one of the top sellers.

"Ingersoll wasted his effort. His book is out of print and all but forgotten. The Bible outlives its skeptics."[7]

Some reacted with delay: They procrastinated. It is dangerous to postpone such an important decision. The Bible disparages those who are interested in the gospel but never make a decision, "always learning but never able to acknowledge the truth" (2 Tim. 3:7). Since tomorrow is unknown, you may never hear the gospel presented again, or may never have an opportunity to respond again. Even more tragic, the attitude of your heart may never be the same again. Repeated denials of Christ's claim on you may callous your heart against the voice of the Holy Spirit. No wonder Paul cries out, "As God's fellow workers we urge you not to receive God's grace in vain. For he says, 'In the time of my favor I heard you, and in the day of salvation I helped you.' I tell you, now is the time of God's favor, now is the day of salvation" (2 Cor. 6:1-2). Don't delay your response to Christ!

Some reacted with decision: They believed. There's no way to fail by preaching Jesus and the Resurrection. God used that mighty message to reach some hungering, searching hearts. "Whoever believes in him is not condemned" (John

3:18). "If you confess with your mouth, 'Jesus is Lord,' and believe in your heart that God raised him from the dead, you will be saved" (Rom. 10:9).

Dionysius was one who responded and believed. At one time he had been mayor of Athens and was now a member of the great court on Mars' Hill. Though beyond 60 years of age, his heart rejoiced to find life in Christ. No doubt he was an important influence in the development of the church in Athens. One ancient historian asserts he became the bishop of Athens. Even though he was up in years and held a distinguished office, he knelt humbly at the cross of Jesus and was born again. Jesus did what Greek views of philosophy could not do—deal with the sins and guilt of the past once for all. What joy to know your sins are forgiven!

Five hundred years after Paul's sermon on Mars' Hill, the Parthenon was converted into a Christian church and was used for Christian worship for more than 1,000 years. Paul's testimony rings through the ages, "For I am not ashamed of the gospel of Christ: for it is the power of God unto salvation to every one that believeth; to the Jew first, and also to the Greek" (Rom. 1:16, KJV). Thank the Lord; the Unknown God is knowable!

During the Columbia Exposition many years ago, representatives from different world religions presented claims for their faiths to guests at the fair. Ten men spoke for a short time about the essential claims of his own religion.

The last speaker was a Christian. After all the philosophic proclamations by the others, the Christian simply told the story of Lady Macbeth, the woman who had connived the murder of King Duncan of Scotland.

Lady Macbeth had not actually committed murder, but in that intriguing Shakespearean drama, she was responsible. King Duncan had died and was buried, but no one knew who his assassins were. No one knew how Lady Macbeth was involved—no one, says Shakespeare, except Lady Macbeth. She knew, and the wickedness of the murder in her heart began to eat away at her spirit. The secret locked up in her began to affect her life and her mind.

She became deranged, incoherent at times. People who knew her best worried about her. One night, as she paced the floor of her room, a small group of acquaintances outside her door listened to her in great concern. In her agonizing delirium, she saw what no one else could—the blood of the king on her hands.

She opened up the secrets of her conscience that night until the whole underhanded affair was known to her listeners on the other side of her wall. "Blood, blood! Oh, oh, oh, blood!" she screamed. "All the perfume in Arabia can't make my hands clean again!"

After telling that story, the spokesman for Christianity turned to the people behind him on the platform and asked, "What does your religion offer Lady Macbeth?" No one had an answer.

Then, with convincing effect, he quoted 1 John 1:9—"If we confess our sins, he is faithful and just, and will forgive our sins and cleanse us from all unrighteousness" (RSV).

Christ knows all about us, yet He forgives and cleanses us so that the stains of sin are removed from our lives—forever! Someday we will stand in God's presence. The books that hold the panorama of our lives will be open; and for those who have trusted Jesus, there won't be a mark or spot against us on any page: not a sin, not an impurity, not an evil thought, not a misdeed. Across the account, we can write:

Jesus paid it all;
All to Him I owe.
Sin had left a crimson stain;
He washed it white as snow.

—Elvina M. Hall

2

When I Feel like Quitting

Acts 18:1-22

Have you ever felt like quitting? At one time or another, circumstances, pressures, or broken dreams may make us waver on the brink of quitting moral and spiritual ideals. Sometimes we begin to think the light at the end of the tunnel is a train coming the other way.

Many years ago, completely discouraged, a prospector swung his pick high over his head, drove it deep into the ground, and said, "I quit!" And he walked away from years of hard labor.

Several years later, someone found a rich vein of gold only 11 feet beyond that abandoned pick. Discouragement persuaded the old prospector to quit too soon.

If Columbus had quit and turned back, no one would have blamed him—but no one would have remembered him either!

On a rainy day, a man came home and found a dog on his doorstep. As he entered, the dog sneaked in behind him. The man put the dog outside in the rain. Later, when his son came home from school, the dog came in and was immediately escorted out again. When the newsboy delivered the paper, that dog slipped in as the father opened the front door. Once again, he was ejected.

Sitting down to read his newspaper, the father began to think of the little dog out in the rain. Admiring the dog's persistence, the man decided his son should have a pet. Downstairs he found an old crib easily converted for the dog's bed. Going back upstairs, the man opened the door—but no dog! He whistled, but no response.

If that dog had only tried one more time, he would have found a nice warm home, a soft bed, and a boy to play with.

You may *feel* like quitting—but don't quit too soon! You might miss one of the greatest opportunities of your life.

That's Paul's mood in Acts 18. Having sensed God's call to preach in Europe, Paul and his team immediately sailed to Macedonia. Though there had been many conversions, Paul had gotten jailed, beaten up, and ridiculed. Going on to Athens to preach to "reasonable" men, Paul found them largely underwhelmed by his sermonic attempt to reveal their "Unknown God." Like many people, they preferred to leave God unknown rather than to know Him and to obey Him.

Paul left Athens, walking the 40 lonely miles west to Corinth, Roman capital of Achaia. Desolate, Paul may have wondered if this business of preaching was worth it. Experiences of his second missionary tour had been taxing. With an uncertain future, Paul found himself alone in the land of Greece, a people advanced in culture and science.

Before Jesus' birth, Greeks believed the earth was round. To them, nature's perfect shape was the sphere—that's why the Supreme Being made the earth round. During a lunar eclipse, their scholars noted that the earth formed a circular shadow on the moon.

About 240 B.C., a Greek geographer calculated the size of the earth. Working in Alexandria, Egypt, on the day the noonday sun is farthest north, he discovered that a vertical stick cast a seven-degree shadow. At that exact time, the sun was directly overhead at Aswan. Noting the seven-degree angle difference and the distance from Alexandria to Aswan, he figured that the world is 25,000 miles in circumference. Seventeen centuries later, he was proved correct.

In 129 B.C., a total eclipse of the sun occurred at the Hellespont, modern Dardanelles. During the same solar eclipse, only 80 percent of the sun was obscured in Alexandria. By studying the distance and the angle, Hipparchus calculated that the moon is 240,000 miles from Earth.[1]

Corinth, the Bridge of Greece, sits where Greece is almost cut in two by the sea, a narrow piece of land four miles wide or less. Most commercial traffic passed through Corinth, so it became the site of many historic battles. In 150 B.C., Roman general Mummius destroyed the glory of old Corinth filled with arts and grandeur that leisure promotes. When Julius Caesar in 46 B.C. declared it the site of a Roman colony, a boom-town sprang up on the ashes of art galleries and crumbled statuary.

The new and noisy Corinth went after money. Eager Italians looked for easy fortunes, while Greek merchants competed with Jews flocking in with their commercial skills, along with their bigotry, strange cultural customs, and exasperating self-assertiveness. Wherever Jew met Greek, there was confrontation. Old citizens of Corinth abhorred Jewish synagogues springing up. However, Romans allowed their subjects to worship anything, anywhere, as long as worshipers were contented and Roman peace was not disturbed.

Corinthian brass became famous. The Isthmian Games, held every fourth year, drew huge crowds of competitors and spectators. Corinth became a cosmopolitan melting pot where "anything goes." The temple of Aphrodite, world-famous cult of sexual promiscuity, had 1,000 religious prostitutes working the streets of Corinth. As Athens had a reputation for culture, Corinth had a reputation for corruption. The phrase "to live like a Corinthian" described a life of luxury and immorality. In Greek drama, characters from Corinth were typecast as drunk.

Paul found himself in Corinth as part-time preacher and full-time tent and sail maker to pay expenses. He faced skirmishes with Jews because he was a Christian, with Greeks because he was a Jew, and with Romans because his disputes often blocked traffic and distracted customers. In the midst of all that conflict, many Corinthians turned to Jesus and were baptized.

Perhaps discouraged by opposition and possible danger to his life, Paul may have had thoughts of quitting or leaving Corinth. Obviously, Paul had some low moments, for he wrote to the Corinthians later: "I came to you in weakness and fear, and with much trembling" (1 Cor. 2:3).

Luke continues the story: "One night the Lord spoke to Paul in a vision: 'Do not be afraid; keep on speaking, do not be silent. For I am with you, and no one is going to attack and harm you, because I have many people in this city'" (vv. 9-10). God knew how Paul felt. He gave Paul the boost he needed at the right time. What a tremendous message from God: "Don't be afraid! Speak out! Don't quit!" (v. 9, TLB).

No matter how discouraged you may become, no matter how much you doubt your effectiveness, no matter how many other things seem more important, keep on and don't quit. The Bible tells us, "The Lord knows how to rescue godly men from trials" (2 Pet. 2:9).

When you feel like quitting, remember God has the same word for you and me as He did for Paul.

When I Feel like Quitting, God Has a Word of Courage

"Do not be afraid; keep on speaking, do not be silent" (v. 9). When God says, "Do not be afraid," He urges us not to give in to fear and depression. We can take to heart too keenly the sense of seeming failure and isolation. When we feel like quitting, we usually have things out of perspective: "Dismiss your fears" (v. 9, Weymouth).

Many years ago Woody Hayes coached football at Ohio's Denison and Miami universities. When he became head coach at Ohio State University, Woody was overwhelmed at first. He said, "The first time I stood in the middle of . . . OSU stadium with its 86,000 seats staring down at me, I was shook up. My young son was with me and had hold of my hand. He must have felt my reaction, for he said, 'But, Daddy, the football field is the same size.'"

Woody Hayes had gotten his eyes on people instead of on his assignment for which he had trained. How easily we get things out of perspective! When we feel like quitting, we are not seeing things correctly. Napoleon learned, "True genius in war is the one who can do the average things when those around him grow hysterical with emotion or fright." God's Word says, "Have no fear" (v. 9, NEB).

Everyone faces setbacks and disappointments in life. But "disappointments should be cremated, not embalmed!" The Lord says, "Stop being afraid" (v. 9, Williams). In response to God's word of courage, pray: "Lord, help me to remember that nothing will happen to me today that You and I together can't handle."

The Lord encouraged Paul: "Keep on speaking, do not be silent." Put in a good word for the Lord. In a moment of human weakness, we are tempted to curb our witness when words seem to have no effect. We often give in to a Polaroid psychology, expecting instant results. But life is not like that. "Speak out! Don't quit!" Silence is not always golden; sometimes it's just plain yellow!

The Lord encouraged Paul: "Keep on . . . do not give up" (v. 9, Goodspeed). Keep on keeping on! When you feel like quitting, you are looking for proverbial greener pastures. However, John Burroughs wrote, "The lure of the distant and the difficult is deceptive. The great opportunity is where you are."

When I Feel like Quitting, God Has a Word of Promise

"Do not be afraid; keep on speaking, do not be silent. For I am with you" (vv. 9-10). God's command was followed by a promise: "For I am with you." People may oppose Paul, but the Lord stood by him. Later Paul testified, "If God is for us, who can be against us?" (Rom. 8:31).

At His ascension, Jesus promised the Church: "And, lo, I am with you alway" (Matt. 28:20, KJV). And now Jesus gave Paul personal assurance: "For I am with you." Jesus Christ offers His personal attention to each one. His presence makes the difference.

A little girl on her way to kindergarten was hit by the neighborhood bully, Butch. She went home crying, "Daddy, take me to school so that Butch won't hit me."

The following day the father took her by the hand, and they walked together to school unharmed. Her fears of Butch subsided. After several days, the girl announced, "Daddy, I guess Butch is gone. I can go to school on my own. I won't need you." Off she went unguarded; and without warning Butch pounced on her. He had not gone away. Butch knew he did not dare bother her while her father walked with her. The moment she walked alone, Butch attacked again.

In our relationship with Jesus Christ, we are totally dependent upon Him. Satan has no control over us, nor can he defeat us, as long as we walk with the Lord. Bill Bright said, "As we abide in Him, and He remains at the control (center) of our lives, we can be assured of victory over every enemy" of our mind and spirit.[2]

When we feel like quitting, the Lord's presence strengthens us, His love encourages us, and His hand reaches out to steady us!

David Livingstone returned from 16 years in Africa. His body was thin and bony after 27 fever attacks. An arm hung useless from a lion's bite. Before a student audience, he asked, "Shall I tell you what sustained me amidst the toil, and hardship, and loneliness of my exiled life? It was the promise, 'Lo, I am with you alway, even unto the end.'"

Jesus promises to be near, even when we don't sense His presence. He walks with us, even in our darkest moments.

Caesar sent a message to General Cicero, who was facing the danger of defeat: "Caesar to Cicero: Keep up your spirits. Expect help!" Cicero was strengthened by that word of promise. He kept on, help came, and Cicero was victorious.

My friends, keep up your spirits. Expect help. Believe God; He is able! Faith is believing God and acting like it. Let's act like we believe God and do what God leads us to do. God envelops us with His Holy Spirit, not to save us from pressure, but to make us strong in the midst of pressure.

When I Feel like Quitting, God Has a Word of Victory

"For I am with you, and no one is going to attack and harm you, because I have many people in this city" (v. 10). Sometimes our view gets swallowed up with problems and pains until we forget to notice our assets and friends. Before deciding to quit, let God help us tally up the sheet honestly.

A man went to Charles Allen, pastor of First Methodist Church in Houston. The visitor had considered suicide because he felt he had lost everything. Since he had lost his business and every dollar to his name, he felt he had no reason to live.

The pastor took a paper and drew a line down the center. On one side he wrote, Losses. On the other column he put, Assets. The pastor jotted down under Losses, "business" and "money." Then he asked, "Have you lost anything else?"

The forlorn man replied, "No; but that's everything!"

"Has your wife left you?" the minister inquired.

"Oh, no," the man assured him. "She still loves me. And she has a job in a department store to help out."

Under Assets the pastor listed "wife" and "wife's job." He asked about his children. The man had two, and both were loyal to him. The pastor wrote "children" under Assets.

Had the visitor forgotten all he learned in 25 years of business? Of course not! In fact, he knew much more now than when he started. The pastor listed under Assets, "knowledge" and "experience."

His next question probed, "Is there as much opportunity today as 25 years ago?" The distraught man assured the minister that there was much more opportunity today. Under Assets they put down "opportunity." His health was good, so "health" was listed next. Did he believe in God? He did, so "God" was written down as an Asset.

Charles Allen admitted it wouldn't be easy to lose a business you've worked 25 years to build. But instead of concentrating on his losses, they talked about concentrating on his assets. A man with a loving wife, loyal children, knowledge, 25 years of experience, opportunity, health, and God should be able to say with Mr. Hopeful in *Pilgrim's Progress* at a dark river in life: "Be of good cheer, my brother; the bottom is sound!"

The man left, having realized he did have firm foundations on which to build again. He went out with "good cheer" in his heart.

When we need it most, God gives a word of victory. The Bible says, "The good man does not escape all troubles—he has them too. But the Lord helps him in each and every one" (Ps. 34:19, TLB). Life in Christ is not automatically a bed of roses nor a guarantee of unruffled serenity. But He promises to be with us, and nothing in creation can separate us from Him (Rom. 8:38-39). Later Paul wrote back to his Corinthian brothers: "Therefore we do not lose heart. . . . For our light and momentary troubles are achieving for us an eternal glory that far outweighs them all" (2 Cor. 4:16-17).

God's ultimate purposes would not be halted by Paul's opposition and obstacles. God had some jewels tucked away in the cesspool of Corinth. Amid the city's corruption, God had both men and women living unspotted lives for Jesus and knew of many others who would be won through the clear witness of the believers: "I have many people in this city." People like Priscilla and Aquila were influencing others for Christ. God was at work. Men may interrupt Paul's service, but they could not interfere with God's ultimate purpose. That note of victory breathed courage into Paul.

When we feel like quitting, let's remember that God and His people shall ultimately win. God promises victory, right in the nick of time. When we consider quitting, God reveals a little more of His eternal triumph. The more we trust God, the more strength we receive to be faithful. In following our Lord, we are linked to a born winner.

If we listen to Jesus, He brings triumph out of tragedy. He took Paul at a low ebb and gave him victory. While staying in Corinth, of all places, Paul wrote the First and Second Thessalonian letters, probably the letter to the Galatians, and very likely his greatest work, the letter to the Romans. Who can guess how God works things out?

A young lady went through college and entered seminary, preparing to be a missionary. But her sister died, leaving three small children. The young lady quit school and gave the next 15 years of her life to those children. She had good reason to question. However, the children all grew up and volunteered for missionary work. God needed three missionaries instead of one.

Pointing to the Congo River, David Livingstone often asked the natives of the African interior, "Where does your great river go?"

They always answered, "It is lost in the sands." They had never seen the great sea to which their river made its way. They just assumed it came to nothing in the sand.

When we feel like quitting, we may wonder, "Where does all my life and labor and effort go?" In moods of discouragement and fatigue, the answer comes, "It is lost in the sand."

But Jesus' victory brings to our ears the roar of the distant sea, and we are assured that our life and labor and efforts are not lost in the sands of time. If you've begun to wonder if it's worth keeping on, hear God's word once again: "Don't be afraid! . . . Keep on . . . Don't quit! . . . For I am with you, and no one is going to . . . harm you."

Ike Skelton was a student at Wentworth Academy in Missouri. At 13 he was striken with polio. For weeks he was paralyzed and in a coma. Doctors offered no hope. But Ike would not give up. He believed God was his Friend and Helper. Ike finally recovered with no permanent damage to his organs except that both arms were paralyzed, completely useless. They just limply hung down.

Though Ike loved sports, he knew he was now limited to track. He could still run. To everyone's surprise, Ike went out for the track team, signing up for the two-mile run. You could see him after school, determined, arms flopping uselessly at his sides, plodding hour after hour, day after day. Ike worked hard to build up his wind capacity and leg strength.

Not until the season's last meet had Ike built up enough stamina. Kemper Academy was their archrival, and this was to be Ike's first race. When the day came, Ike entered the two-mile run. At the starting line, the coach slit open Ike's track pants and taped one useless arm to his bare leg. The other arm was tucked in the pocket of his jacket.

The gun sounded, and the boys were off. Spectators watched that determined young Ike Skelton. He never wavered or faltered. Ike crossed the finish line and was hoisted on the shoulders of his ecstatic teammates amid the biggest ovation of the day.

Ike didn't win first place. He didn't come in second or third. In fact, Ike finished last—one lap behind everyone else. But Ike's personal victory was the greatest triumph! He kept going when it was easy to quit.

"Wherefore seeing we also are compassed about with so great a cloud of witnesses, let us lay aside every weight, and the sin which doth so easily beset us, and let us run with patience the race that is set before us, looking unto Jesus the author and finisher of our faith" (Heb. 12:1-2, KJV).

3

The Secret of Victorious Living

Acts 18:23—19:41

A young man said to his pastor, "Religion for my grandfather was an experience, for my father it was a tradition, and for me it is a nuisance!"

Somewhere between the first and second generation, the joyful note of victory was lost. The victorious life faded into the traditions of keeping the church going. The dynamic Spirit of God was lost in the shuffle.

Dr. Alan Redpath, British pastor and Bible teacher, spent 10 years in the United States as pastor of Moody Memorial Church in Chicago. He traveled widely as a popular speaker at Bible conferences from coast to coast. When he returned to Scotland, he shared his impressions of American Christianity. While impressed favorably with evangelistic outreach and missionary giving, Dr. Redpath noted:

"I have observed a very real hunger of heart among a great number of Christians in this land for the fullness of the blessing that God has for them in Jesus Christ. Many Christians are highly dissatisfied with their lives; are conscious of defeat and frustration and long to enter into a deeper experience of what union with Christ . . . really means in terms of practical daily conduct."

He added, "Far too many Christians have lived exceedingly long on the right side of Easter but on the wrong side of Pentecost, on the right side of forgiveness but on the wrong side of fellowship, on the right side of pardon but on the wrong side of power.

"To use an Old Testament allegory, they are 'out of Egypt' but not yet in the 'land of full salvation.' Many have wandered in the wilderness—and in the carnality of Romans 7 instead of in the conquest of Romans 8."[1]

Missionary Paul found the same situation when he began his ministry in the city of Ephesus. The busy seaport and western terminal of the trade route to the Euphrates had about 250,000 people. Ranked with Antioch in Syria and Alexandria in Egypt as one of the three great eastern Mediterranean cities, Ephesus eventually disappeared when the river silted up. The harbor became a marsh, and the people relocated to escape malaria. In Paul's time, Ephesus contained one of the Seven Wonders of the World—the temple of Artemis or Diana. The glory of pagan Ephesus is but a dim memory with only a few fragments of broken marble left in the dirt.

After leaving Corinth, Paul visited Ephesus on his way to Antioch, concluding his second missionary tour. Paul left his friends Priscilla and Aquila in Ephesus and promised to return. He was gone about a year. During that year something happened in Ephesus—the coming of Apollos: "Meanwhile a Jew named Apollos, a native of Alexandria, came to Ephesus. He was a learned man, with a thorough knowledge of the Scriptures. He had been instructed in the way of the Lord, and he spoke with great fervor and taught about Jesus accurately, though he knew only the baptism of John. He began to speak boldly in the synagogue" (18:24-26). Apollos had gone through formal training in Alexandria about Jesus and the Scriptures. He may have studied some of the Christian writings that had begun to circulate. Apollos was an eloquent speaker.

"When Priscilla and Aquila heard him, they invited him to their home and explained to him the way of God more adequately" (18:26). Apollos knew about the life and teachings of Jesus, about His death and resurrection; but he had either not known or not experienced the dynamic power of the Holy Spirit. He had not yet encountered a personal Pentecost. That's the secret to victorious living! From that moment on, Apollos' ministry was never the same. Encouraged by the brethren and empowered by the Holy Spirit, Apollos went on to Corinth to preach.

"While Apollos was at Corinth, Paul took the road through the interior and arrived at Ephesus" (19:1). Paul stayed in Ephesus from autumn of A.D. 52 until spring of 55. He remained in Ephesus longer than at any other place during his active ministry. As a result, Paul used Ephesus as the center of his third missionary tour. The Roman province of Asia was so thoroughly Christianized by Paul and his team that for centuries the churches there were among the most influential in the world. In fact, their churches survived Turkish conquest until the Greek-Turkish war in 1923 when populations were exchanged.

During Paul's stay, he wrote at least four important letters to Corinth from Ephesus, two of which exist in our New Testament. Paul founded a great church to which Timothy later was appointed as pastor. According to tradition, the apostle John brought Mary, mother of Jesus, to spend her last days in Ephesus.

As far as Luke's record goes, Ephesus was Paul's last work as a free man. Shortly after leaving Ephesus, we'll find Paul imprisoned or under guard to the end of the Book of Acts.

What did Paul find when he arrived in Ephesus? "There he found some disciples and asked them, 'Did you receive the Holy Spirit when [or 'after,' margin] you believed?'

"They answered, 'No, we have not even heard that there is a Holy Spirit.'

"So Paul asked, 'Then what baptism did you receive?'

"'John's baptism,' they replied.

"Paul said, 'John's baptism was a baptism of repentance. He told the people to believe in the one coming after him, that is, in Jesus.' On hearing this, they were baptized into the name of the Lord Jesus. When Paul placed his hands on them, the Holy Spirit came on them, and they spoke in ['other languages,' margin] and prophesied. There were about twelve men in all" (19:1-7).

Probably these 12 disciples were the imperfect results of Apollos' incomplete preaching. Like Apollos, they had not received the Holy Spirit: "No, we have not even heard that there is a Holy Spirit" (19:2). These 12 good men were saved. If Abraham was justified by faith hundreds of years before Jesus came (Romans 4), those who repented of sin and believed on the coming of Messiah, as John the Baptist had preached, would be saved. Luke calls them "disciples," a common term for Christians.

Christians today resemble the 12 disciples in Ephesus more than they do the 12 disciples in Jerusalem after Pentecost. We know the facts, the history, the Bible, and the traditions. We have a grateful sense of forgiveness—but where's the power? Where's the dynamic Spirit of God? Where's the added dimension of the Holy Spirit instead of the "falling down" believer? It's sad that powerless Christianity sits around debating whether or not one can lose his salvation instead of asking, "How can I receive the power of the Holy Spirit?"

Paul didn't ask about their standing in the community. He didn't ask if they liked their preacher or had adequate buildings. He never asked about their records or financial stability or membership list. Paul didn't even ask if there were any spiritual "Achans" in the camp or if they were straight theologically. Uppermost in Paul's mind was the question, "Did you receive the Holy Spirit [after, since] you believed?"

Dr. William Greathouse noted, "This question underscores the theme of the Acts. . . . For this reason Acts has been . . . called by some the *Acts of the Holy Spirit.* Within the few pages of this earliest church history we are confronted by no less than fifty-seven references to the Spirit; the entire book is a commentary on the person and work of the Holy Spirit."[2]

Maybe you have wondered, "Why has my religion not made a more vital difference to me? Why don't I experience victorious living as a Christian? Why don't I ever see any results of being a Christian?" God's Word asks you today, "Did you receive the Holy Spirit [since] you believed?"

Perhaps you are saying, "But I've tried and tried to be a good Christian. Something's missing!" Personal striving, "trying harder," is not the answer. Apollos and others before him had left those good men in Ephesus straining and striving, an achieving type of sub-Christianity! That's not the full gospel of grace through Jesus Christ.

James S. Stewart said, "Wasn't it too bad of those who taught them the rudiments of the Christian faith—to leave those poor innocents in their little boat with nothing but oars! Not telling them that they might step a mast and let loose a sail, for there was always a favoring breath on the face of those waters!"[3]

To you straining on the oars trying to be "Christian," the most important question the Bible raises for the disciple of Jesus is this: "Did you receive the Holy Spirit [since] you believed?" That's the secret of victorious living. I have three important questions.

For Victorious Living, Have You Received the Holy Spirit?

Those 12 Ephesian disciples had repented of their sins: "John's baptism was a baptism of repentance" (19:4). Apollos and the 12 men had been baptized unto repentance. They might have been baptized by John the Baptist, and if so, it had been 26 years earlier. However, it may mean they were baptized into John's emphasis on repentance. According to Ray Stedman, "John declared three great truths: First, . . . forgiveness of sins is possible before God only on the basis of repentance. . . .

"[Second] John had the people express their repentance in baptism . . . a symbolic act of cleansing. . . .

"Third, John announced that One was coming who would complete the work he had begun. Repentance is just a beginning with God."[4]

John's ministry brought people to repentance and remission of sins. Baptism is the outward symbol that our sins have been washed away.

Apollos and the 12 men were eager to learn about Jesus. They believed in the Christ John preached. They held no resistence to learning more about Jesus. But they had not yet been baptized with the Holy Spirit. George Mueller said that the night God's Spirit filled him, he learned more in four hours about the Scriptures than he'd learned in the preceding four years since becoming a Christian.

Apollos and the 12 men were living for Jesus. They possessed Christ but were not possessed by Christ. Imitating the life of Jesus is not adequate. It isn't enough to know something about Jesus and to try to follow Him. That's why the Sermon on the Mount seems to many people to be impossible!

The Holy Spirit is not optional equipment. He is the Secret to victorious living. Apart from the Holy Spirit, these disciples were simply enthusiastic advocates of Jesus. They could speak with feeling about the Carpenter from Nazareth, the great Teacher, the best Man who ever lived. They knew all about Jesus' life, death, and resurrection; but they had no comprehension of the indwelling Christ at Pentecost. These men had walked in all the light they had received, had repented and believed, had separated themselves from the world, and may have suffered persecution.

However, they had not received the fullness of the Holy Spirit. Until you have your personal Pentecost, you can only partially understand what God has done through the coming of the Holy Spirit. The Ephesian disciples had only an inadequate and incomplete grasp of God's grace. Perhaps Paul noted the inadequacy and incompetency in their assignment in pagan Ephesus. They had obviously made no significant impact for Christ.

How tragic to stand in the pulpit like that Sunday after Sunday, year in and year out, with nothing vital to say; to teach a Sunday School class without firsthand experience to draw upon; to head up a young people's organization, yet live a morally defeated life; to be the father of a family and a leader in the church, but behave at home so that his children mock religion!

Churches abound. Religious activity goes on. Never has the church had better facilities and more people. But our great need is the power of the Holy Spirit—the living, energizing, revolutionizing power that moved so mightily in the disciples after Pentecost! "Did you receive the Holy Spirit [since] you believed?" Millions of Christians are good, but empty! How about you?

For Victorious Living, Did You Know That the Holy Spirit Is Available?

"Did you receive the Holy Spirit [since] you believed?" One writer noted, "The grammatical construction of this question (in the original Greek) permits it to be translated either 'since you believed' or 'when you believed.' Translators therefore tend to follow their theological bias."[5]

It's interesting that theological debates rage over whether Paul said "since you believed" or "when you believed." As Dr. J. B. Chapman pointed out, "In either case their answer was

No. . . . They knew nothing of the infilling and indwelling of the divine Comforter. . . . The gift of the Spirit is the lost note in modern Christianity."[6]

The 12 Ephesian disciples, as Apollos, did not know that God had given the promised Holy Spirit: "No, we have not even heard that there is a Holy Spirit" (19:2). Henry Jowett said, "How imperfect their equipment! How inadequate their resources! . . . The day of Pentecost had come; the marvelous promises had been fulfilled; the wonder ministry had begun; but these disciples were still in the pre-Pentecostal days; they were behind the spiritual times." It's impossible to imagine the Early Church without Pentecost!

Christian proclamation is no longer "only the Messiahship of Jesus, but the indwelling power of the Lord. The Christian life [is] not just living for Jesus, but Christ living in the believer."[7]

Those Ephesian believers did not know of any divine enablement. While John baptized with water, he pointed to the day when Christ would baptize with the Holy Spirit and with fire. The first baptism was the washing away of a sinful past; the second baptism was God's gift of power to lead a pure life. That's why divine enablement is necessary. The Christian needs the internal presence of God to experience victorious living.

A gospel based on human striving rather than divine enabling devastates the child of God. We must have Him who is God's great Gift!

The Ephesian disciples did not know that the Holy Spirit was available. If they had heard of the Holy Spirit coming upon the apostles many years earlier at Pentecost, they had no idea He was available for them.

They were like many people today for whom Christianity is similar to courtship. It is always trying to put its best foot forward; it is striving toward some desired future goal. That's the stage in which we awaken to our own inadequacies. The more we try to do better, the more we invaribly fail because we're attempting victorious living in our own strength. Courtship is an inner struggle.

However, God intends Christian experience to be similar to marriage. We are the Bride of Christ, resting in a relationship already attained. No more timidity and tension and uncertainty; we belong to Him. There's the joy of exploration and development in the secure commitment of marriage. That's the stage when we discover that our condemnation is taken away. We are enabled to do in the power of the Holy Spirit what we could never do or be in ourselves. That's victorious living!

The Holy Spirit is available to all disciples of Jesus. We can partake of His Spirit and nature, which makes holiness of heart possible. We love and appreciate the Jesus of history but need to experience "the glorious riches of this mystery, which is Christ in you, the hope of glory" (Col. 1:27).

The Holy Spirit is as available to us as He was to the disciples in Jerusalem and to the disciples in Ephesus. When the Ephesian Christians heard about the Holy Spirit, they were eager to receive Him.

For Victorious Living, Will You Be Filled with the Holy Spirit?

Paul took the disciples of Apollos' incomplete ministry and unfolded the full dimension of God's plan in the Cross, the Resurrection, and Pentecost. "On hearing this, they were baptized into the name of the Lord Jesus. When Paul placed his hands on them, the Holy Spirit came on them" (19:5-6).

Suddenly those 12 disciples experienced an Ephesian Pentecost. And a new outpouring of the Holy Spirit will come to any people who ask and seek for Him. It's one thing to believe in the Holy Spirit, but quite another thing to receive the Holy Spirit. God's Spirit is available to you today. Jesus made it clear: "If you then, though you are evil, know how to give good gifts to your children, how much more will your Father in heaven give the Holy Spirit to those who ask him!" (Luke 11:13).

Will you be filled with the Holy Spirit? If you are a Christian, you are eligible to receive the Holy Spirit.

First, to be filled with the Holy Spirit, you must desire Him. The Ephesian disciples obviously wanted Him.

Harold Ivan Smith told of a friend who had custody of his two sons after an unpleasant divorce. The boys spent a weekend before Christmas with their mother and her family. They were showered with gifts. When the boys returned home, they noticed a barren Christmas tree. They asked, "Dad, what are you going to give us?"

The father, with his boys in the middle of their lavish gifts, had to search for the right words. It was an awkward moment. "Boys, the only thing I have to give you is myself. That's not much, but it is all I have to give. I promise I'll never leave you. I'll always try to be here when you need me, in July as well as at Christmas."

After a moment of thoughtful silence, both boys climbed over the gifts and hugged their father: "We love you, Daddy. You're all we want!"[8]

Do you want the Holy Spirit's gift of himself? He'll never leave you nor forsake you. He'll be there all the time—for richer, for poorer; in sickness and in health.

Second, to be filled with the Holy Spirit, you must surrender to Him. Churches today are filled with people who know the gospel of Jesus and who try to live good, moral, Christian lives; but they have never given up directing their own lives. They are saved but not surrendered. That stifles God's Spirit working through His people.

Augustine said, "I don't know whether I have lost my will, or whether at last my will is so much like God's will that I cannot tell which is my will and which is God's will. But I know that I will to do God's will."

That's surrender. That's submission at its best. That's complete consecration. That kind of total surrender to God's will brings His response in cleansing power.

Third, to be filled with the Holy Spirit, you must accept Him by faith. Jesus said, "Receive the Holy Spirit" (John 20:22). Trust Him to keep His promise! Jesus said, "I will ask the Father, and he will give you another Counselor to be with you forever—the Spirit of truth" (John 14:16-17). You need nothing more than the promise of Christ. Take Him by faith!

Fourth, to be filled with the Holy Spirit, you must be receptive to Him. The Holy Spirit never forces himself into your life. He awaits your response. You either accept Him or reject Him. The Ephesian disciples eagerly received Him, and "the Holy Spirit came on them."

Catherine Marshall described her need of the Holy Spirit and her response to Him: "My heart needs to be cleansed and set in order for such a royal Guest. I give You permission now to prepare my inner being. And, Lord, help me to be open and receptive!" That must be your attitude toward the Holy Spirit.

Open your heart to the light of God's Spirit. Let Him show you what He will. Flowers don't open because they try hard. It's the natural result when exposed to sunshine and rain. The life of holiness is not by straining and struggling, but by openness to God's Word and being receptive to the Holy Spirit. "Did you receive the Holy Spirit [since] you believed?" Today, the most important question remains, "Will you be filled with the Holy Spirit?"

When the Ephesian disciples were given opportunity, they had the greatest revival recorded in the New Testament since the Day of Pentecost. A three months' revival shook the synagogue (19:8-9). "God did extraordinary miracles through Paul" (19:11). Paul opened a holiness school for two years (19:10). "Many of those who believed now came and openly confessed their evil deeds. A number who practiced sorcery brought their scrolls together and burned them publicly"

(19:18-19). God's Word began spreading and gaining power in their part of the world (19:20). Christians took Ephesus so completely for Christ that the idol-makers supplying the tourist trade coming to visit the temple of Diana suffered a lack of business. The silversmiths held a protest rally (19:23-41)! What a revival it must have been! Ephesus became the outstanding New Testament church of that era.

Paul wrote back to them later, "Be filled with the Spirit" (Eph. 5:18). The Greek text does not simply mean, "Be filled with the Spirit once for all, and that's the end of it." It suggests, "Remain continuously filled." Keep on living the Spirit-filled life! That's the secret of victorious living. Let this prayer fill your heart:

Hover o'er me, Holy Spirit,
Bathe my trembling heart and brow;
Fill me with Thy hallowed presence,
Come, O come and fill me now.

Thou canst fill me, gracious Spirit,
Though I cannot tell Thee how;
But I need Thee, greatly need Thee;
Come, O come and fill me now.

—Elwood H. Stokes

4

Till We Meet Again

Acts 20:1-38

After shepherding the church in Ephesus for three years, Paul continued on his third missionary tour, going to Macedonia: "He traveled through that area, speaking many words of encouragement to the people, and finally arrived in Greece, where he stayed three months" (vv. 2-3). Luke compressed one year of Paul's ministry into that one sentence. Writing to Christians in Rome, Paul said that he preached for that year in Illyricum (15:19), later known as Dalmatia and today as Yugoslavia. In Paul's three-month residence in Greece, he wrote his letter to the Romans, his most important and comprehensive writing.

A group of delegates began a pilgrimage with Paul to visit Jerusalem for the annual Feast of Pentecost. Sailing from Macedonia, they landed in Troas, birthplace of Paul's God-given vision to evangelize Macedonia (chap. 16). Probably delays due to unfavorable sailing weather kept them in Troas for a week. On Sunday evening, Paul and the delegates met with Christians in Troas for a service. Paul preached past midnight. A young fellow named Eutychus, sitting in the window, fell asleep, Luke says, "sinking into a deep sleep as Paul talked on and on" (v. 9).

Sleeping in church is an old problem. One preacher said, "Most congregations are evenly divided between those who are sound asleep and those who want to go home!" One thing I remember about my parents: They did their sleeping at home. They never used the sanctuary for an adult nursery! Luke, who was in the room, noted: "There were many lamps in the upstairs room where we were meeting" (v. 8). As Dr. William McCumber wrote, "Sometimes people fall asleep in church as the victims of poor ventilation. The brain doesn't get enough oxygen. And sometimes people sleep in church as victims of poor preaching, which can't be helped by simply opening a window. It requires the harder work of opening a mind."[1]

Burning lamps past midnight may have caused Eutychus to fall asleep during Paul's sermon, but today burning television tubes past midnight Saturday or all Sunday afternoon causes many people to sleep in church. Evan Esar said, "A good religious sermon helps people in different ways. Some rise from it strengthened; others wake from it refreshed!"

Going out the window during a sermon is one thing; but from the third floor? That's ridiculous! "When he was sound asleep, he fell to the ground from the third story and was picked up dead. Paul went down, threw himself on the young man and put his arms around him. 'Don't be alarmed,' he said. 'He's alive!' Then he went upstairs again and broke bread and ate. After talking until daylight, he left. The people took the young man home alive and were greatly comforted" (vv. 9-12).

Paul either preached too long or got so preoccupied that he forgot some of his luggage. Later Paul wrote from Rome for Timothy to bring his cloak and a crate of books and parchments (2 Tim. 4:13).

En route to Jerusalem, Paul and his travelers stopped at Miletus, 30 miles from Ephesus. He called for the elders to come and meet him there on the coast—perhaps the same 12 disciples he first met on his arrival four years earlier.

The *New International Version* headline for verses 13-38 announces: "Paul's Farewell to the Ephesian Elders." As I was lying in bed with my Bible and notebook, working on this passage, my wife leaned over and looked at several potential sermon titles and outlines: "Farewell to Friends" and "A Final Word" were at the top of the list. She turned to me and asked, "Are we leaving our church?"

No, but I have been thinking about life's inevitable farewells. The longer I live, the more often I am having to say, "Farewell," to family and friends. Leaving the home of a longtime fellow pastor and friend dying from a brain tumor, I sensed he had given his last message to his people. Since that heartbreaking farewell, I have wondered, What would be on my heart if I knowingly preached my last sermon?

In a time of evaluation, I came to Paul's famous "Farewell Address" to the Ephesian elders. In it he expressed his deep intimacy as a Christian leader and friend. This is the only recorded message of Paul given to church leaders, the only record in the Book of Acts of Paul speaking to a Christian audience (vv. 17-35). In his farewell, Paul assessed the past, present, and future: a moment of introspection and evaluation, a moment of pouring out his heart to his friends, a moment of simple trust in the reliability of God.

Looking to the Past, Paul Speaks of a Clear Conscience

Paul was saying, "I did my best for you as I understood it." A clear conscience is a soft pillow. What a wonderful thing to be able to look back without regret! Listen to Paul's defense of his ministry among them.

First, Paul said, "I served the Lord with great humility" (v. 19). Humility is not worm-crawling self-abasement nor pompous self-aggrandizement. Humility is honest assessment of oneself. Paul knew who he was in the Lord, and he knew God had called him to give his best. He had performed faithfully. Whether others thought so or not, Paul knew he had been a good steward of his opportunities. After all, one should be more concerned about what his own conscience whispers than what other people shout!

A church was looking for a pastor. The Pulpit Committee sifted through applications, and the clerk read them aloud one by one. It seemed all candidates had high moral character, were brilliant orators, tireless pastors, experts at reviving stagnant churches, and could make misers give gladly.

That is, all except one applicant. He was different from the others: "I have preached in a number of small churches, mostly located in big cities. I have never been in one place for more than three years. I have had some success as an author. My relationships with certain religious officials have not always been the best. Some of these office-bearers actually threatened me. I have been in jail three or four times for disturbing the peace. I am over 50 years of age, and my health isn't very good. My memory is so poor that I have been known to forget the names of people I've baptized. Nevertheless, I still get quite a lot done. If you appoint me, I'll do my best for you."

The moderator of the Pulpit Committee exclaimed, "What? Appoint an unhealthy, trouble-making, absent-minded jailbird? Who does he think he is?"

The clerk replied, "Well, sir, he signs himself, 'Paul.'"

Second, Paul added, "I served the Lord . . . with tears" (v. 19). He was tough-skinned but tenderhearted. His compassionate attitude showed how deeply he felt his people's needs. During his Ephesian pastorate (chap. 19), Paul sorrowed over those who hardened their hearts against God's message (19:9). He sorrowed over those who exploited the message of Christ for personal gain (19:13). He sorrowed over those who opposed the Good News—Demetrius and his silversmith friends, suffering from decreased idol-making trade.

Paul reminded the Ephesian Christians, "I have been with you at all seasons" (20:18, KJV). He was not a fair-weather friend but had suffered with them through all their experiences. Paul had urged, "Rejoice with those who rejoice; mourn with those who mourn" (Rom. 12:15), and he practiced what he preached. That builds the pastor-people relationships.

Third, Paul, with a clear conscience, could say, "I have not hesitated to preach anything that would be helpful to you" (v. 20). Or, "I kept back nothing" (KJV). The Greek word for "kept back" is a nautical term for reefing sails. He had watched sailors many times shorten their sails in order to go slower or more cautiously under storm. Paul was saying to his friends, "I have put on all the sails. I have been open to every breath of the Holy Spirit. I have done everything to bring the church to the 'harbor.'" "Harbor" in the Greek is the origin of the word "grace." He had reserved nothing. Whatever would have been for the people's good, Paul preached boldly. Sails are hoisted not for display but for power. Sermons must do the same. Truth must not be softened to make the good news of Jesus seem easy or comfortable. Paul never held back in his preaching to please the tastes of his people, but gave them what they needed.

Fourth, Paul added, "But [I] have taught you publicly and from house to house" (v. 20). What Paul was in the pulpit, he was wherever he went. Paul did his best to demonstrate God's truth at all times.

Fifth, Paul said, "I have declared to both Jews and Greeks that they must turn to God in repentance and have faith in our Lord Jesus" (v. 21). He did not favor one group over another. As pastor of all segments of his church, he applied the same message to all. Paul kept talking about repentance before God and faith in Christ. Everyone needed it.

Sixth, Paul's selflessness shows up in his statement, "I consider my life worth nothing to me, if only I may finish the race and complete the task the Lord Jesus has given me—the task of testifying to the gospel of God's grace" (v. 24). Here's a man with a cross, a man with a ministry, a man unashamedly testifying to the goodness and glory of God. He would do anything for Jesus. Would you? "Life is worth nothing unless I use it for doing the work assigned me by the Lord Jesus" (v. 24, TLB).

Seventh, Paul states emphatically, "I declare to you today that I am innocent of the blood of all men. For I have not hesitated to proclaim to you the whole will of God" (vv. 26-27). He had presented the full-orbed good news of Jesus. Not only does God save but also He sanctifies and keeps! Not only are sins forgiven but also our hearts can be cleansed from all sin. Not only should we repent of wrong but also we should have faith in the daily, delightful walk in the power and presence of the Holy Spirit.

Failure to tell the whole story—the Cross, the Resurrection, and the filling with the Holy Spirit—leaves sincere, searching Christians caught up in the "failure-repentance-failure" cycle. God offers deliverance. Paul testified: "What a wretched man I am! Who will rescue me from this body of death? Thanks be to God—through Jesus Christ our Lord! . . . Therefore, there is now no condemnation for those who are in Christ Jesus" (Rom. 7:24—8:1). Paul had been faithful to "tell it like it is." He had faithfully discharged his responsibility to the Ephesians. They were without excuse.

Entering the presidency of the United States, Abraham Lincoln declared: "I desire to so conduct the affairs of this administration that if, at the end, when I come to lay down the reins of power, I have lost every other friend on earth, I shall have at least one friend left—and that friend shall be down inside me!"

When a person has done his best with limited understanding and judgment and has used the tools and opportunities open to him, he need not have regrets. He can face God with a sense of assurance and a clear conscience.

Looking to the Present, Paul Speaks of a Great Challenge

Paul was saying, "Do your best to serve God!" He had given his best in the past, but now it was up to the Ephesian Christians. Paul was passing the torch of leadership to the Ephesian elders. His past work now rested in their hands. Paul gave them three challenges for the present.

First, Paul challenged: "Be on guard for yourselves" (v. 28, NASB). They must first be diligent in their own souls. You cannot minister successfully to others until your own heart is blessed by the presence of God. Your first responsibility is the watchful care over your own spiritual life. How difficult that can be under pressures to be available to everyone as needed, under pressures of meetings and appointments from early morning until late at night. But your relationship with God is top priority, over all other legitimate calls and demands.

Jesus pleaded, "Be careful, or your hearts will be weighed down with . . . the anxieties of life, and that day will close on you unexpectedly like a trap" (Luke 21:34). Paul warned Christians of Corinth, "So, if you think you are standing firm, be careful that you don't fall!" (1 Cor. 10:12). Once Paul sent a message urging, "Tell Archippus: 'See to it that you complete the work you have received in the Lord'" (Col. 4:17).

Second, Paul challenged: "Be on guard for . . . all the flock, among which the Holy Spirit has made you overseers, to shepherd the church of God which He purchased with His own blood" (v. 28, NASB). Elders must give diligent care to the church. Christian leaders must intuitively have an eye for careless sheep. A flock can scatter as each one nibbles himself lost. Shepherds learn how to keep them together, heading in one direction.

One day I found an old basketball and took it to a church member's dog—an Australian sheepdog. He has that natural instinct to herd and guide sheep to wherever his master leads.

In absence of sheep, he keeps in practice with a basketball. You can't kick the ball far enough away for him not to be able to herd it back to your feet.

As I watched him in action, I thought about what a church could be with 15 elders who know how to bring and keep our people at the feet of Jesus. Overseers should work diligently and carefully because the flock has been bought by the precious blood of Christ. The Ephesian elders took the challenge so seriously that the church at Ephesus became the foremost church during the last third of the first century, passing up Jerusalem and Antioch. Even in the second century, decisions made by churches in Rome and Ephesus were considered of prime importance.

Third, Paul challenged: "Remember that for three years I never stopped warning each of you night and day with tears" (v. 31). He didn't want them to forget that compassion for people must burn in their hearts. They should remember how Paul had wept and pleaded for them. Some people may try to disrupt or divide the church or lure it off on some tangent. Dry-eyed, coldhearted, polished, and pampered members will never save the church. The Bible says, "They that sow in tears shall reap in joy. He that goeth forth and weepeth, bearing precious seed, shall doubtless come again with rejoicing, bringing his sheaves with him" (Ps. 126:5-6, KJV).

The strength of Paul's example sprang from his capacity to bring out the best in people. Leaders needed the same expectations in the flock as Paul had had in them. He was saying, "Never stop believing in what God can do in people!"

At Johns Hopkins University, a sociology class studied one of the worst slums in Baltimore. Cards were tabulated on the people in that section. Among the cards, 200 were marked, "Headed for jail." Each card had a brief sketch of background, attitudes toward life, and the prospects that indicated the person was probably headed for jail. The report was filed in the university's archives.

Twenty-five years later another sociology class found this survey of 200 boys and girls, black and white, "headed for jail." As a project, the class checked every card and investigated what had happened.

The first card led them to a physician in Baltimore. The student investigators asked him, "You were listed as incorrigible, 'headed for jail.' What happened?"

The doctor confessed, "I was the worst kid in the neighborhood, but Aunt Hannah changed all that."

"Who is Aunt Hannah?"

She was a teacher in the slums. One day she invited him for Sunday dinner. Aunt Hannah told him, "Joe, I've been studying you. I've discovered that with your hands you have the capacity to be a terrific surgeon. I forsee the time when you'll be one of the great men of medicine in Baltimore. I'm going to follow you, Joe, all the way."

The doctor remarked, "I walked out of Aunt Hannah's house, feeling I couldn't let her down. I remember saying to myself, 'She sees me as a great surgeon. What do you know?' So I missed jail because of Aunt Hannah."

The sociology students went to the manager of a huge supermarket. They asked, "You're on the list. How come you didn't make it to jail?"

He replied, "I used to steal stuff for a gang out of the grocery store on this very location. I finally got caught, but providentially I talked to Aunt Hannah. She pointed out that when we do something wrong, we must pay for it some way. Was I willing to pay back all I had stolen? I was—and Aunt Hannah worked it out with the grocer and the police.

"I worked in the grocery store and paid back all the money. I liked working there. One day Aunt Hannah said to me, 'You're going to run one of the biggest grocery stores in Baltimore. What do you think?' She believed in me and helped me believe in myself. Finally I bought the store and improved it and enlarged it. This very site is where I stole food and was headed for jail. But Aunt Hannah changed all that. She saw something in me!"

The sociology class discovered only 2 out of 200 "headed for jail" ever got there. Why? Aunt Hannah! She saw something special in them. She impressed them with the idea that they were called to be children of God, designed to stand tall and walk straight, to master their circumstances. By God's help, she gave them hope.

Paul challenges us to work diligently for the Lord in this present day.

Looking to the Future, Paul Speaks of a Strong Confidence

Paul was saying, "God will see you through!" Yes, the sands of time were running out. The irreversible years were marching on. But Paul had confidence in the future, for the future belongs to God. God is in control. Paul expressed confidence in four ways.

First, with confidence, Paul said to his friends, "Now I commit you to God" (v. 32). "I commit" or "I commend" (KJV) is an old verb meaning "to deposit in a bank for safekeeping." Paul must leave, but he would deposit them in the care and security of God, who had kept him also.

Later, in Paul's last letter to Timothy, pastor at Ephesus, he wrote, "I know whom I have believed, and am convinced that he is able to guard what I have entrusted to him for that day. . . . Guard the good deposit that was entrusted to you—guard it with the help of the Holy Spirit who lives in us" (2 Tim. 1:12, 14).

John Wesley wrote a letter to a pastor retiring after a long ministry: "Be of good cheer! He who took care of the sheep before you were born will not forget them when you are dead!"

Second, with confidence, Paul said to his friends, "I commit you . . . to the word of his grace" (v. 32). The age-old question rings yet today, "Is there any word from the Lord?" (Jer. 37:17). God's Word of grace—the Holy Scriptures—has the answer. Grace is God's love in action. God's grace is always for the undeserving. I can entrust you to God's future because His grace always reaches out for all who are so unworthy.

God's Word of grace is foreign to many people who serve a harsh, uncaring God. What a beautiful surprise they have coming!

A mother unwisely used the fear of God to discipline her boy. When he would get restless, she'd say, "God won't like that." When unruly, "God will be angry." Usually that was enough to control him.

One night she served prunes on his plate. He didn't want any. She coaxed, pleaded, and finally threatened: "God won't like this. God doesn't like little boys who refuse to finish all their prunes."

He remained steadfast. For some reason he refused to eat the last two prunes on his plate—dark, wrinkled tokens of his rebellion.

At her wits' end, she demanded, "You must go to bed. You've been a naughty boy, and God is angry!"

No sooner had she tucked him in bed and come back down to the kitchen than a violent thunderstorm broke loose. Lightning thrashed around more vividly than usual. Thunder clattered with rolling reverberations. Angry winds threw handfuls of rain against the windows.

She rushed upstairs, knowing her boy would be terrified, hiding under the covers. Instead, he was at the window with his face pressed against the glass. She heard him mutter, "My, my, such a big fuss to make over two little prunes!"

That's some people's idea of God. How little do many folk comprehend God's great works of grace—all because He loves us so much. Yes, I commend you to God's word of grace, for His grace is sufficient.

Third, with confidence, Paul said to his friends, "I commit you . . . to the word of his grace, which can build you up" (v. 32). No one has arrived. There's no room for arrested development in the heart of a Christian. God's Word keeps adding to our spiritual fortress block by block, a course at a time—upbuilding God's kingdom in our hearts by faith. God continues building us up line upon line, precept upon precept. Don't get discouraged; God isn't through with you yet.

A boy was asleep in his backyard one afternoon. A helicopter pilot had been surveying the area. Spotting the sleeping boy, the playful pilot came down quite low and shouted over the megaphone, "Hang in there!"

The lad jumped up and rushed into the house frightened. But that's Paul's word to his Ephesian friends: "Hang in there!" God will see you through.

Fourth, with confidence, Paul said to his friends, "[God will] give you an inheritance among all those who are sanctified" (v. 32). The gift of the Holy Spirit is God's down payment on our inheritance as His children. Every Christian has the privilege of an incorruptible, undefiled, glorious crown of life that never fades. "Eye hath not seen, nor ear heard, neither have entered into the heart of man, the things which God hath prepared for them that love him" (1 Cor. 2:9, KJV).

James S. Stewart concludes, "The promised inheritance . . . stands . . . with Christ's own promise to guarantee it. 'Enter into the joy of your Lord!' The One who spoke these words is here today. . . . He is present now. . . . 'Come, ye blessed of my Father, inherit the kingdom!'"[2]

Paul's "Farewell Address" was marked by his statement: "Now I know that none of you among whom I have gone about preaching the kingdom will ever see me again" (v. 25). When he finished, they prayed together, hugged each other, and walked Paul to the awaiting boat.

There's always a note of sadness about a last time. Unspoken memories must have flooded them. Unutterable prayers must have been offered. But that's the spirit in which every sermon should be preached and received. We will never meet exactly like this again with the same people and the same opportunities. This moment can never be repeated. Express your love and worship now.

It's no wonder Richard Baxter said he preached as a dying man to dying men. There is a changing pageantry of people. We have only this moment to help and encourage each other in the Lord.

Separations are a part of this life, but fellow Christians never say, "Good-bye," for the last time. We never have to say a final farewell. Take hold of the glorious promise of reunion in God's home where we'll never have to say, "Good-bye," again. The old song says it well:

God be with you till we meet again;
By His counsels guide, uphold you;
With His sheep securely fold you.
God be with you till we meet again.

—Jeremiah E. Rankin

5

Up to Your Ears in Alligators

Acts 21:1—23:11

At one time or another most of us have felt like the fellow who was told to go drain the swamp—and found himself up to his ears in alligators! Now, that's a lot of trouble! Sometimes it seems that if anything could go wrong, it already has.

Finding herself in exasperating circumstances, one woman exclaimed, "It seems as if every time I pick up a piece of string, I find an elephant attached to it!"

Norman Vincent Peale noted, "A physician remarked that about half of the people who come into his office do not actually have anything physically wrong—they've just had the life knocked out of them."[1]

Acts 21 through Acts 23 finds the apostle Paul up to his ears in alligators. He's really in a swamp of trouble. The little traveling preacher goes from bad to worse, from the frying pan into the fire, until he just about has the life knocked out of him.

After a fruitful ministry in Ephesus, how could things get so bad for Paul so quickly? Paul had decided to go to Jerusalem. He always had a burning desire to win his brethren, the Jews, to Jesus Christ. However, he overlooked a clear command of the Lord to which he testifies in chapter 22: "When

I returned to Jerusalem and was praying at the temple, I fell into a trance and saw the Lord speaking. 'Quick!' he said to me. 'Leave Jerusalem immediately, because they will not accept your testimony about me'" (vv. 17-18).

That's plain enough: "Get out of Jerusalem!" God seems to be saying to Paul, "What are you doing in the Temple? I have abandoned it; the veil has been torn in two. Get out of Jerusalem and stay out!" In fact, Paul admits, "Then the Lord said to me, 'Go; I will send you far away to the Gentiles'" (22:21).

In disregarding God's earlier instructions, Paul, by returning to Jerusalem, was bound to get into trouble. People told him it was dangerous, but he felt a compulsion from his compassion for unsaved Jews.

During Spain's Civil War, in one of the skirmishes some of the men considered surrender. One comrade spoke up, "I'd rather die on my feet than live on my knees!" Paul was that kind of man.

The traveling delegation sailed a route that sounds like an Aegean Sea cruise itinerary. The ship anchored at Cos, a small island off the southwest tip of Asia Minor. It was the home of a well-known medical school and the home of Hippocrates, the father of medicine.

The next day they landed at Rhodes, the "island of Roses," on the southwest coast of Asia Minor. A statue of Colossus, 105 feet tall, had been built in 280 B.C., one of the Seven Wonders of the World. Cicero and Julius Caesar had studied at Rhodes.

The next landfall was Patara, a seaport famous for its oracle of Apollo.

Their sailing ship came to rest in the great Phoenician seaport of Tyre, then in Syria, now part of Lebanon. During a week's delay in Tyre, Luke notes: "Finding the disciples there, we stayed with them seven days. Through the Spirit they urged Paul not to go on to Jerusalem. But when our time was up, we left and continued on our way" (21:4-5). Once more the Holy Spirit was urging, "Paul, don't go to Jerusalem. Change your plans!" But Paul felt compelled to go.

They sailed 25 miles south along the Israeli coastline to Ptolemais, now known as Acre. Only eight miles north of Mount Carmel, at the head of the Bay of Acre, it is the Old Testament city of Accho, where Solomon maintained a chariot city like Har Meggido.

At last, Paul and his crew arrived in Caesarea, capital of Israel. The Lord is so patient; He sent another roadblock to Paul. Agabus, a prophet from Jerusalem, "took Paul's belt, tied his own hands and feet with it and said, 'The Holy Spirit says, "In this way the Jews of Jerusalem will bind the owner of this belt and will hand him over to the Gentiles."'

"When we heard this, we and the people there pleaded with Paul not to go up to Jerusalem. Then Paul answered, . . . 'I am ready not only to be bound, but also to die in Jerusalem for the name of the Lord Jesus.' When he would not be dissuaded, we gave up and said, 'The Lord's will be done'" (21:11-14).

Paul would not budge in his determination.

When friends begged Martin Luther not to go to the Diet of Worms, he responded, "Though devils be as many in Worms as tiles on the roofs, yet there I will go!" Facing blatant opposition, Luther declared, "Here I stand; I can do no other!" That's the spirit of Paul setting his course to Jerusalem, good sense or not.

As it turned out, this was Paul's last visit to Jerusalem. Dr. DeHaan asked, "Why did not the Lord stop Paul? He could have taken him home to glory or prevented him in some way from continuing in his . . . determination. . . . God . . . was going to demonstrate His abounding grace in making Paul's mistake the occasion for a great and wonderful ministry after he reached Rome. Yes, God can cause even the wrath of man to praise Him. And so in the purpose and plan of God,

He overruled Paul's willfulness and turned it into the greatest ministry of Paul—the writing of the Prison Epistles to the churches while he spent his closing days 'a prisoner of the Lord Jesus Christ.' . . . It did not excuse Paul, but it does magnify the grace of God."[2]

Arriving in Jerusalem, Paul delivered the offering to the church that had been sent by the Gentile churches. The Jerusalem church had become fatigued by persecution and famine. It seems they were in a holding pattern, having lost their aggressiveness. By their suggestion, Paul entered the Temple to carry out certain religious Jewish rites. When Paul was recognized by pilgrims from the province of Asia, chaos broke loose. The Jews viewed Paul as a traitor. The crowd tearing at Paul got shoved out of the Temple gates to prevent bloodshed in the Temple. His compromise with the Jews turned out very sour. "Peace at any price" wasn't the answer then, and it isn't today.

Romans would not tolerate civil disturbance. Soldiers were alerted and sent to quell the riot. The outcome was that Paul was beaten up by the crowd, arrested by the Roman soldiers, and imprisoned. In chains, he spoke to the people who listened intently until he admitted that God had sent him to preach the good news of Jesus to Gentiles. That sparked the multitude into hot anger. They shouted, "Rid the earth of him! He's not fit to live!" (22:22).

When the Roman garrison prepared to flog Paul, he pulled out the fact of his Roman citizenship, and that began a legal process that would eventually take him before Caesar.

The next day Paul faced the Jewish Sanhedrin, but when they got unruly, he cleverly divided the members of the Sanhedrin over the issue of resurrection from the dead. It was a classic tactic. When the uproar settled, Paul was left in prison under Roman guard.

As DeHaan commented, "Paul's good intentions landed him in jail. Paul's public ministry is ended, and the rest of the story in Acts is a record of Paul's trial, his journey to Rome, and ends with Paul in prison. All his efforts at appeasement, compromise, concession and cooperation were of no avail."[3]

In this dark section of the Book of Acts, one verse shines above the rest: "The following night the Lord stood near Paul and said, 'Take courage! As you have testified about me in Jerusalem, so you must also testify in Rome'" (23:11). When Paul was up to his ears in alligators, God came to Him in a wonderful way. We can learn from Paul's experience how to deal with times of trouble.

In Times of Trouble, Look for God's Involvement with Your Life

Luke said it so well: "The Lord stood near."

The Lord stood by Paul, not to save him *from* danger, but to save him *in* danger. All that mob violence had a familiar ring echoing in the streets of Jerusalem nearly 30 years earlier. Yes, the Lord understood Paul's experiences. Jesus, too, had been beaten, rejected, scorned, and broken in Jerusalem. "The Lord stood near Paul." The living Christ knew how much Paul needed someone to stand by with him.

During the last assault against the German army in World War II, General Eisenhower walked beside a soldier marching to the Rhine. Ike could detect fear and uncertainty in the young man. The soldier had been wounded and had just returned to the front lines, nervous, tense, filled with fear.

The general said, "Son, you and I should be good for each other. I am nervous, too."

Marching together, Ike, supreme commander of the Allied forces, began to explain the tremendous military machine backing them up. They had forces far superior to the enemy. This assault would be backed up by unimaginable air force superiority.

As they reached the banks of the Rhine River, the soldier remarked, "General, I want to tell you: I *was* nervous, but I'm not now!"

When you face troubles that seem to overwhelm you, rejoice. "For we do not have a high priest who is unable to sympathize with our weaknesses, but we have one who has been tempted in every way, just as we are—yet was without sin. Let us then approach the throne of grace with confidence, so that we may receive mercy and find grace to help us in our time of need" (Heb. 4:15-16).

Paul learned what we must discover: Jesus keeps His word. He will not desert His people. Jesus promised, "I will not leave you as orphans; I will come to you" (John 14:18).

Jerry Adams was a bomber pilot during the Vietnam War. One day the three-man bomber was ordered to a bombing mission. As they were catapulted off the ship, the plane broke, and they fell into the sea. From the flight deck to the water is about 70 feet, equivalent to a seven-story fall. The plane sank quickly to a depth of about 50 feet of water. Jerry had difficulty getting loose but finally made it to the surface—just in time to see the ship bearing down on them. Though he could be cut in two, the ship went past, and the men were rescued—the only time a three-man crew was rescued during the Vietnam War.

Jerry testified later, "At the precise moment when the aircraft was catapulted from the ship and broke apart, I felt Jesus by my side. I could see Him; He put His arm around me. He didn't say to me that my life was going to be spared, but He gave me assurance that no matter what happened, I needn't be afraid, that He would take care of me all the way. From that flashing moment I knew that I did not need to be afraid of anything, either in life or death; that the Lord Jesus Christ would be with me always."

Paul wrote of his glorious hope, "For I am convinced that neither death nor life, neither angels nor demons, neither the present nor the future, nor any powers, neither height nor depth, nor anything else in all creation, will be able to separate us from the love of God that is in Christ Jesus our Lord" (Rom. 8:38-39).

Jesus himself will stand by you though all the troubles of life be hurled at you. You can depend on Him! You will find the presence of Christ.

In Times of Trouble, Look for God's Inspiration in Your Life

The Lord standing by Paul said, "Take courage!"

Things were looking bleak for Paul until Jesus spoke, "Take courage!" That single Greek word is the same word Jesus had spoken to the paralytic (Matt. 9:2), the hemorrhaging woman (Matt. 9:22), the disciples in the boat during the terrible storm (Matt. 14:27), the blind man (Mark 10:49), the discouraged disciples at the Last Supper (John 16:33)—and He speaks to us the same word: "Take courage!"

Paul needed a boost. Everything had gone wrong, and he was in serious trouble. But Jesus could say to his spirit of dejection, "Be of good cheer!" While Paul thought he was doing the right thing, he had to lick his wounds of failure. The Lord knew Paul's motives were pure and good, in spite of failure. God would use Paul's witness for our good and God's glory.

Even when you are up to your ears in alligators, God has a word of peace for your spirit. His peace garrisons the soul. An Indian once said, "Let me pray, not to be sheltered from dangers, but to be fearless in facing them."

After a devastating air raid on Britain in World War II, an inscription was found on a small new grave: "There is not enough darkness in all the world to put out the light of one small candle." In moments of trouble, of discouragement, of defeat, or of despair, you will find the peace that Jesus gives: "Take courage!"

I look not back—God knows the fruitless efforts,
The wasted hours, the sinning and regrets;
I leave them all with Him who blots the record
And graciously forgives and then forgets.

I look not forward—God sees all the future,
The road that, short or long, will lead me home;
And He will face with me its every trial,
And bear for me the burdens that may come.

But I look up—into the face of Jesus!
For there my heart can rest, my fears are stilled;
And there is joy, and love, and light for darkness,
And perfect peace, and every hope fulfilled.

—J. H. Hunt

Paul could testify: "God is faithful; he will not let you be tempted beyond what you can bear. But when you are tempted, he will also provide a way out so that you can stand up under it" (1 Cor. 10:13).

Friends, even though trouble comes, "Take courage!"

In Times of Trouble, Look for God's Intent for Your Life

The Lord standing by Paul said, "As you have testified about me in Jerusalem, so you must also testify in Rome."

The Master had a word to calm Paul's fear about the future. God wanted Paul "in Rome." And we must not let the future breed in us uncertainty. As we follow our Lord faithfully, we will make every one of God's appointments. When Christ reigns in our hearts, we always face a bright tomorrow! No wonder a biographer of Albert Schweitzer said he was a man "less concerned with happiness than with purpose." To be happy isn't important, but to find God's intent and plan is the sure way to fulfillment; and happiness becomes a welcome by-product.

By Acts 23, Paul was probably around 60 years of age. Far from being on the shelf, God intended to use Paul to transfer the center of the gospel work from Jerusalem to Rome. Behind the curtain of the future, in only 8 more years the war would begin in which Rome would crush and destroy Jerusalem, A.D. 66-70. The Jews would cease to be a nation until the fulfillment of the prophesied return in 1948, re-creating the state of Israel. God would use Paul's trip to Rome in part as a transfer of Christendom from Judea to Rome, the center of the empire.

At 65 years of age, when most men plan retirement, Winston Churchill came to power in Great Britain. Norway and Denmark had already fallen to Nazi Germany. The war monster was about to swallow up Belgium and Holland. France was peering down the throats of the first German Panzers. As Churchill drove along the Mall to Buckingham Palace to receive the king's commission as prime minister, he knew of the crumbling military fronts, the lost battles, the dwindling hope. What were his thoughts? "I was conscious of a profound sense of relief. At last I had the authority to give directions over the whole scene. I felt as if I were walking with Destiny, and that all my past life had been but a preparation for this hour and for this trial."[4]

And all of Paul's past life was culminating in the upcoming assignment to preach in Rome, capital of the known world. Sitting in that jail, Paul was walking with destiny, indeed!

It was pointed out, "The fulfillment of God's promise that Paul would get to Rome took a long time. Many weary months of imprisonment and difficulty intervened. Just as many an American youth, unable to afford travel abroad, has seen the world after joining the Navy or the Marines, so Paul would get to Rome at last—at the expense of the Roman government."[5]

When you're up to your ears in alligators, when trouble seems to sweep in on you, look for God's intent. You will find the plan of Christ. One writer noted, "Though God may reveal some distant outlines of the shape of our life to come, for the most part His will is revealed in the now. He gives us enough insight into the future to set a course, but our day by day walk within His will is more like a scroll than a blueprint. A scroll is rolled on two sticks. If you want to read the scroll, you unroll a little on the right stick as you roll up a little on the left. Things get all messed up if you unroll the entire scroll."[6]

Cease meddling with God's plan and will;
You touch anything of His and you mar the work.
You may move the hands of the clock to suit you,
but you do not change the time.
You may hurry the unfolding of God's will,
but you harm and do not help the work.
You can open a rosebud, but you spoil the flower.
Leave all to Him. "Thy will, not mine."[7]

The Bible says, "In everything you do, put God first, and he will direct you and crown your efforts with success" (Prov. 3:6, TLB). But we measure our success by God's intent and plan for our lives. Our great troubles are often necessary preparation for greater duties up ahead! Look for God's long-range intent beyond the present moment of trouble. Someone said, "More dreams, poems, high inspirations, and rare insights have been born in prisons and on beds of suffering than in all the vacation spots!"

If God has permitted troubles to come our way, we can be sure He has thought His way through all of them. He never goes off on a tangent. He never makes up His mind before considering all the facts. If we do His will, God can outwit any situation. When God calls us, we can rest assured that perfect obedience will result in a perfect solution. "If God be for us, who can be against us?" (Rom. 8:31, KJV).

When you are up to your ears in alligators, the Lord will be standing near. Somewhere in the shadows, you will find Him. "Take courage!" Look for God's long-range goals; that will keep you from being frustrated by short-range failures. Never judge life by any one experience through which you are passing. God is still working all things together for good.

We would do well to adopt E. Stanley Jones's motto for life: "When life kicks you, let it kick you forward!"

6

Life's Great Tragedy

Acts 23:12—24:27

Ralph Waldo Emerson wrote, "We are always getting ready to live, but never living."

Psychologist William Moulton Marston quizzed 3,000 persons: "What have you to live for?"

He was shocked to find that 94 percent were simply enduring the present while they waited for the future, waiting for "something" to happen: waiting for the children to grow up and leave home, waiting for next year, waiting for some long-dreamed-about trip, waiting for someone to die, waiting for tomorrow—without realizing that we only have today, because yesterday is gone and tomorrow never comes.

Herein lies life's great tragedy: putting off life until later. Great decisions are postponed to some more convenient day. Satan's supreme scheme for destroying people is procrastination, a fault most people put off trying to correct.

At Bedford Springs, Pa., Dr. William Paxton talked with then president of the United States, James Buchanan, about Jesus and the claims of the gospel. At the conclusion of their discussion, the president said he believed Christianity was true, and when he finished his term of office, he would make a confession of faith.

Dr. Paxton replied, "But, Mr. President, the gospel says, 'Today,' not 'Tomorrow.' 'Now is the accepted time'" (2 Cor. 6:2, KJV).

Satan doesn't care how spiritual your intentions or how holy your resolutions if only they are fixed on "tomorrow."

Life's great tragedy is illustrated by Antonius Felix, governor of Judea, as he faced the apostle Paul.

While Paul was imprisoned in the Roman fortress in Jerusalem, more than 40 Jews vowed to neither eat nor drink until they killed Paul. Paul's nephew overheard the plot and reported to the Roman commander. Immediately the officer, Claudius Lysias, told his centurions, "Get ready a detachment of two hundred soldiers, seventy horsemen and two hundred spearmen to go to Caesarea at nine tonight. Provide mounts for Paul so that he may be taken safely to Governor Felix" (23:23-24).

Claudius sent a letter to the governor: "Greetings. This man was seized by the Jews and they were about to kill him, but I came with my troops and rescued him, for I had learned that he is a Roman citizen. I wanted to know why they were accusing him, so I brought him to their Sanhedrin. I found that the accusation had to do with questions about their law, but there was no charge against him that deserved death or imprisonment. When I was informed of a plot to be carried out against the man, I sent him to you at once. I also ordered his accusers to present to you their case against him" (23: 26-30).

In darkness of night, Paul was escorted from Jerusalem to Caesarea, a 60-mile ride to the seacoast. When the governor got the letter, he put Paul under guard at Herod's palace. Ordinarily a trial date must be set for no more than three days; but allowing for a messenger's two-day trip and the two-day return with Paul's accusers, the trial was set to begin in five days.

As a Roman citizen, Paul was tried in a Roman court according to Roman law and rules of procedure. Felix was the judge. High Priest Ananias came as prosecutor, bringing Tertullus, a lawyer. Paul acted as his own defender. The proceedings were conducted in Latin, court language of the Roman Empire.

Felix had been born a slave, but his brother, Pallas, had influential friends. Eventually Pallas received an appointment as executive of the Roman Imperial Treasury by the emperor. By Pallas's help, Felix was appointed governor of Judea in A.D. 52. However, Nero became emperor on October 13, 54. Within his first year, Nero removed Pallas from office. Four years later Nero recalled Felix to Rome, removing him from office also.

Tacitus the historian said of Felix, "He exercised the authority of a king with the mind of a slave." Chains may be removed from his hands, but the chains remain on his mind.

Traditionally when a slave became a free man, he would take a new name. This slave-king chose Felix, meaning "happy." Josephus portrays Felix as greedy for money. No wonder he held Paul for two years in prison, hoping for a bribe. Though many edicts came from Rome prohibiting bribery, "the wheels of Roman law . . . ran smoothly and rapidly if they were judiciously greased."[1]

There they stood, face-to-face: Felix, born a slave, wearing a crown; Paul, born free, wearing chains. Official accusations were treason, heresy, and sacrilege. Paul dealt with each accusation with clarity and reason. Felix finally adjourned the trial and announced he would decide later. "He ordered the centurion to keep Paul under guard but to give him some freedom and permit his friends to take care of his needs" (24:23).

A few days later, Felix brought Paul before him and his wife, Drusilla. She was the youngest of three daughters of Herod Agrippa I. He was the Herod who killed James, brother of John. Her great-uncle, Herod Antipas, murdered John the Baptist. Her great-grandfather, Herod the Great, attempted to destroy the newborn Messiah, Jesus, by slaughtering all the babies in Bethlehem. Drusilla had been married off at the usual age of 12 to a little-known king of Asia Minor. Felix persuaded her away from her husband to marry him when she was 16. Now, at age 20, she sat with Felix and listened to the apostle Paul. They knew he was no ordinary prisoner.

No one had a better opportunity for eternal life than Felix and his wife. God sent them a preacher. He turned their audience chamber into a sanctuary. The world was shut out. Nobody dared interrupt. In the power of the Holy Spirit, Paul presented Christ. The heavens were open above. God spoke through His man. Who ever had a better opportunity? The hour of God's grace had struck. The door of the Kingdom was thrown open. The Spirit of God was reaching out to draw them in.

But it all ended in spiritual tragedy, due to postponement. God's offer of eternal life was procrastinated. And it didn't just happen 1,900 years ago. Life's great tragedy happens day after day as men and women say to Christ, "Not now. Some other day, perhaps." From Felix's experience we see the warning signs of spiritual disaster. Perhaps we can recognize them enough to see ourselves.

The First Sign Is Acquaintance Without Acceptance

Luke notes, "Then Felix, who was well acquainted with the Way . . ." (24:22).

Felix knew about Christianity, but he didn't know Christ! He had an acquaintance with ideas and concepts, but he had not accepted Jesus. Believing about Jesus is not the same as believing in Jesus. Felix, like multitudes of churchgoers, was familiar with the Christian religion, but had never personally accepted Jesus as Savior.

Jesus said to one of the world's nicest fellows, "I tell you the truth, no one can see the kingdom of God unless he is born again" (John 3:3). Nicodemus knew all about God and was well-acquainted with Jesus' teachings, but he must personally accept Jesus Christ: "Whoever believes in him is not condemned, but whoever does not believe stands condemned already because he has not believed in the name of God's one and only Son" (John 3:18).

The heart of Christianity is not a philosophy to be learned but a Person to be embraced! Accept God's great gift of eternal life at the hand of Jesus Christ.

The Second Sign Is Interest Without Involvement

Luke wrote, "He [Felix] sent for Paul and listened to him as he spoke about faith in Christ Jesus" (24:24).

Paul didn't just tell the story of Jesus. He aimed the Good News right at the heart of Felix. Paul preached faith! Without doubt, Felix was interested, but Paul preached for a decision —getting involved with the risen Lord. Felix had developed some interest in hearing about God's Word, but God wanted to reach Felix's heart. As Paul preached, Felix stood on the edge of Christianity, looking in. He lingered on the threshold, unable to resist the curiosity to hear about it. But, like a hummingbird, he hovered above the nectar of life, never coming to rest in the sweetness of newborn joy.

Apparently Felix only wanted to hear Paul talk about faith in Christ. But faith cannot be separated from action. It takes more than interest; it takes personal involvement with God's forgiving grace.

Nothing is more heartbreaking than the army of people who settle for a casual interest in Christ and His Church. Their continual refusal to get involved evidences the lack of life-giving reality in their relationship with Christ. Jesus said, "Thus, by their fruit you will recognize them" (Matt. 7:20). The sick barrenness of the uninvolved signals unchanged lives, unforgiven sins, and unsaved well-meaning people.

The Third Sign Is Remorse Without Repentance

Luke wrote, "As Paul discoursed on righteousness, self-control and the judgment to come, Felix was afraid" (24:25).

With the forcefulness of a man called of God, Paul expounded the Christian faith. He drove home the fact that the Christian faith has ethical implications. If you would be Christian, then you must live Christlike. Many people today have a mighty sick and soft idea of what a Christian is. They claim to be Christian while still living in sin. The Bible says, "This is how we know we are in him: Whoever claims to live in him must walk as Jesus did" (1 John 2:5-6). John emphasizes, "Everyone who sins breaks the law; in fact, sin is lawlessness. But you know that he appeared so that he might take away our sins. And in him is no sin. No one who lives in him keeps on sinning. No one who continues to sin has either seen him or known him" (1 John 3:4-6). Sinning sainthood is a myth, a deadly deception.

Speaking on God's behalf, Paul gave a powerful three-point sermon to Felix and Drusilla:

1. God's Ideal for Man: "Righteousness"
2. God's Requirement for Man: "Self-control"
3. God's Assessment of Man: "Judgment to Come"

First, "righteousness" means "right living" as a result of being made right and placed in a right relationship with God. Many people today see themselves as more good than bad, therefore deserving heaven. But our human righteousness is as filthy rags. Only Jesus Christ can place us in a right relationship with God. He is our Savior and Mediator. Only by our personal faith in Jesus can we stand before God. The atonement in Christ is our only plea. Only when our sins are charged to Jesus' account do our lives echo His righteousness.

Second, "self-control" means living in accord with our new status, putting aside our immediate response to every unbridled desire and impulse. As one writer noted, "Because Felix and Drusilla were rulers, they felt they could gratify every impulse of their natures. Many [people] . . . despise the idea of God and do the same thing. . . . 'If it feels good, do it;' and 'Try it—you'll like it!'"[2]

A young woman had been trained in the ethics of Christian living. Against the advice of friends, she joined a traveling troupe of singers who were ungodly people. Two years later she met her pastor. Having taken on most of the ways and habits of her companions, she was a bit self-defensive, saying, "I am just as good as I have ever been."

Soon, however, she dropped the mask of pretense and admitted she had developed terrible moral habits. She said, "I guess that's why I stay up and drink more than I should. I am afraid to go to bed with my conscience!"

Many people have allowed moral sensibilities to grow weak. When God has tried to steady them, they have refused His help. Can you go to bed with your conscience?

Paul's third point emphasized the "judgment to come." What a thrilling climax: "judgment to come." That subject gets deleted from most sermons today. Paul didn't leave it out, nor did Jesus. There's a day of reckoning up ahead. People will reap what they sow (Gal. 6:7). Paul's message to us says, "For we must all appear before the judgment seat of Christ, that each one may receive what is due him for the things done while in the body, whether good or bad" (2 Cor. 5:10). This judgment, though often ignored, is inescapable. People have an amazing capacity to put it out of mind—but only temporarily!

A large number of people at your funeral may indicate your popularity. But by then the only thing that matters is what God thinks of you! Are you ready to face Him?

Looking back on December 7, 1941, "The Pearl Harbor Report demonstrated that not only were an admiral and a general unprepared, the authorities were unprepared and the whole nation was in a lethargy of self-satisfaction. In spite of all the evidence that an attack would come, people were amazed when it did."[3]

The Bible tells of God's judgment to come. It will come as suddenly as a bolt of lightning, as unexpectedly as a thief in the night. But ready or not, His day is coming! Paul's message on the judgment struck Felix's heart and conscience.

Luke says, "Felix was afraid" (v. 25). The Greek word, *emphobos,* means "in fear, startled, terrified, afraid." That's what happened when Felix was confronted with God. But it's not enough to tremble, to be terrified. Remorse for your sins is self-destructive. God calls for repentance, a godly sorrow that leads to a turning away from sin and turning to God. Repentance is a decision to follow Jesus. Paul wanted Felix to turn his life over to the Lord. Judas stopped with remorse—and hung himself. Peter was repentant and returned to fellowship with Jesus.

Don't stop with remorse. Huckleberry Finn said, "Conscience takes up more room than all the rest of a fellow's insides!" Turn your troubled life over to Jesus. His call is always a promotion, a move in the right direction. Any move away from Him is tragic. There's only one way to a bright future, and that is going with Jesus.

Don't settle for conviction without conversion.

Johnny Cash awakened one morning in jail. He had been put there for his own protection. High on pills, Johnny had been looking for inner peace. He had become afraid of everything. Sometimes before a performance he would be almost too sick to go on. Increasingly Johnny would miss appearances for scheduled shows. Here he was, the great Johnny Cash, lying on a jail cot, staring at the ceiling.

The old jailer came to him and told him, "I'm a fan of yours, Johnny. It's a shame to see you ruining yourself. I didn't know you were this bad off." Opening the door for the singer, he added, "Your great talent came from God. You're sure wrecking the body He put it in."

That thought kept reverberating through Johnny's mind. He had never stopped to think that God could help him.

Johnny said, "I asked God to go to work on me right then and there!" God miraculously forgave him and helped him overcome his problem.

Why not let God go to work on you?

The Fourth Sign Is Dismissal Without Decision

Gripped by fear, Felix said to Paul, "That's enough for now! You may leave. When I find it convenient, I will send for you" (24:25). In a mild, polite way, Felix dismissed Paul: "Please be going. When I get some spare time, I'll call you."

In hushing the voice of the preacher, Felix thought he silenced truth. Fatally Felix pushed away God's pleading. Mistakenly Felix assumed he was the one to decide when a time was convenient. He was wrong. Convenient seasons are not ours to grant. We don't order them when we choose. God declared, "My Spirit will not contend with man forever" (Gen. 6:3). Convenient seasons come only by God's mercy. The only convenient season is God's season.

Failure to choose Christ is rejection. Felix said, "When I find it convenient, I will send for you. Don't call me; I'll call you!" But God's Word cannot be reeled in and out at our leisure. Life's great tragedy is to dismiss the Lord without making the decision to follow Him.

A man dreamed he was listening in as Satan talked with some of his demons. They were seeking some new way to trap people. Satan asked, "Who knows how to defeat the souls of men?"

One demon said, "I'll go."

Satan asked, "What will you say to them?"

"I'll persuade them there's no God."

"No," said Satan. "That won't do. The majority will never believe that. They may say so, but in their hearts and in their desperate moments they'll never believe it."

A second volunteer was asked, "What will you do?"

He replied, "I'll persuade them there's no heaven."

"No," said Satan. "Men expect a future life. The instincts of their souls speak of a land of completeness and joy, that land from which we have fallen."

A third demon said, "I'll persuade them that there's no hell."

"No, that won't do it either. You can't persuade them against the pangs of their conscience. We must find something that will appeal to people of all ages, in all conditions, of all beliefs."

A fourth demon whispered, "I'll go."

"And what will you tell them?" Satan asked.

"I'll tell them there is no hurry."

Procrastination is one of the devil's favorite weapons: "Tomorrow! There's no hurry." He doesn't care if you believe in the Good News, as long as you postpone yielding to God's Spirit. Felix blundered, thinking some future time would be better than the present.

There are three big reasons why you should not wait until tomorrow.

First, life is uncertain. Experience points out the frailty of life. Felix's wife and son would die in the eruption of Mount Vesuvius just a few years later.

Second, the power of habit locks you tighter and tighter. Each time we sin, it is more deeply ingrained into our life's pattern. Felix went from bad to worse until he was deposed two years later.

Third, resistance to God's voice becomes easier each time. Dr. George Truett proclaimed, "Every day a soul waits to answer God's call, life gets more complicated, impressions get fainter, convictions get weaker, evil habits get stronger. Inclinations to follow Christ get less and less with every passing day that you resist the Spirit of God. . . . When you resist the Spirit of God, you are sinning willfully. Felix sinned with his eyes open."[4]

That's the reason statistically that most Christians have accepted the Lord in their youth. If God is speaking to you, and if you refuse Him again, it will be more difficult to ever move toward Him again. Don't grieve away the Spirit of God.

Missionary Harry Rich said, "I fully intended to tighten up the wheel lugs on [my] car, but with people coming and going, I forgot and lowered the car. We loaded it and started for the mountains. Five miles later on a bad curve with a two-hundred-foot precipice on one side, I saw my left front wheel disappearing over the cliff. We ground to a halt on the blacktop in time to avoid an accident. No, my good intentions were not enough.

"Billy Sunday preached that the road to hell was paved with good intentions. Many fully intend to become Christians someday, but delay becomes a habit until they cannot break away."[5]

As far as we know, for Governor Felix it was "now" or "never." Though he listened to Paul many times in the next two years, never again was the pull of God so strong. That convenient season never came. Felix destroyed himself by dismissing God's call without a decision.

The affairs of your soul are serious. Strong conviction by the Holy Spirit can be allowed to cool and wear off until, like Felix, spiritual sensitivity has passed. This present moment is your most important opportunity. Make the most of it! In this moment begin your life with Jesus. If God's Spirit has spoken to you, you can never say, "I would have become a Christian if I ever had an opportunity." It's here right now. God's clock doesn't stop. Time keeps running out. We are being weighed in the balances. Few people in hell will have ever expected to be there; decisions were postponed until the unexpected happened! There's no point in gambling with your destiny. Settle it for God today. The time to open your heart's door is when Jesus is knocking; and Jesus knocks at the door of your heart right now.

I urge you by the mercies of God, by the atoning blood of Jesus Christ, by the pleading voice of the Holy Spirit, turn away from Satan's whisper, "Later! Wait a while!" Hear God call, "Behold, now is the accepted time; behold, now is the day of salvation" (2 Cor. 6:2, KJV). The Bible warns, "Today, if you hear his voice, do not harden your hearts" (Heb. 3:15). Avoid life's great tragedy:

"Almost persuaded" now to believe;
"Almost persuaded" Christ to receive;
Seems now some soul to say,
"Go, Spirit, go Thy way.
Some more convenient day
On Thee I'll call."

—Philip P. Bliss

7

Christ at the Crossroads

Acts 25:1—26:32

Christ stands at the crossroads of every person's life. Each one must meet Him alone. That confrontation with Christ, whether brief or in passing, makes the difference in one's destiny.

Many years ago two teenagers entered a little Church of the Nazarene. The message of Jesus was faithfully proclaimed. One youth raised his hand for prayer; the other took it lightly and turned away from Christ. Rejecting Jesus, the young man took a road leading to indecision, prison, divorce, alcohol, and an early death.

The teenager who, at the crossroads, gave his life to Christ attended Olivet Nazarene College (now Olivet Nazarene University), entered the ministry, and has, for more than three decades, been professor of theology at Nazarene Theological Seminary: Dr. J. Kenneth Grider.

While their different roads may seem extreme, their destinations are representative of each person who meets Christ at the crossroads. It *is* the difference between life or death!

Jesus gave good news, saying, "I have come that they may have life, and have it to the full" (John 10:10). Some people say, "I can't believe that a good, loving God will send anyone to hell." I don't believe that either! God doesn't send anyone to hell; people deliberately choose to turn away from Christ. God's whole plan in the Bible through Jesus Christ is to keep people out of hell. In fact, "He is . . . not wanting anyone to perish, but everyone to come to repentance" (2 Pet. 3:9). Christ stands at the crossroads, *pleading* with people *not* to choose hell.

In Acts 25 and 26, God used Paul in chains to bring an imperial governor, a puppet king, and an incestuous woman to Christ at the crossroads.

Felix had prolonged the unfinished business of Paul's Roman trial for two long years. Unexpectedly, Emperor Nero removed Felix from office in the year A.D. 60.

The new governor, Festus, arrived in Caesarea and found a cluttered desk. On his third day in office, Festus traveled to Jerusalem and met the Jewish leaders. Secretly planning an ambush to kill Paul, the religious leaders urged the governor to bring Paul to Jerusalem for a Jewish trial. Festus replied, "Paul is being held at Caesarea, and I myself am going there soon. Let some of your leaders come with me and press charges against the man there, if he has done anything wrong" (25:4-5).

After 8 to 10 days, Festus returned to Caesarea and opened Paul's long-delayed trial. It was another pointless round of unproven charges. Sensing an impasse, Governor Festus attempted to ameliorate the problem by asking Paul, "Are you willing to go up to Jerusalem and stand trial before me there on these charges?" (25:9).

Paul knew about the secret vow of the Jews to kill him. Incensed that Roman justice had bogged down, he refused to return to Jerusalem. Paul finally realized what the Lord meant by His warnings: "Paul, stay away from Jerusalem; don't go near the place, for they will not receive your testimony there."[1] Paul replied, "I am now standing before Caesar's court, where I ought to be tried. I have not done any wrong to the Jews, as you yourself know very well. . . . No one has the right to hand me over to them" (25:10-11).

At that moment, Paul stunned everyone: "Caesarem Appello!" It was an important legal term meaning, "I appeal to Caesar!" (25:11).

As the echo of those words faded, a heavy silence lingered with anticipation. Judge and accusers were startled. The man of destiny once again mastered the storm: "I appeal to Caesar!" Those words brought the hearing to a dramatic close; the proceedings were immediately suspended.

"Caesarem Appello!" These were words of liberty bought by centuries of struggle. A Roman citizen had the right to be heard before his emperor. Modern jurists compare it with the Habeas Corpus Act of English law. Paul had demanded a change of venue to Rome. Festus could neither acquit nor condemn him. He was legally bound to send Paul to Nero, emperor of the Roman Empire.

Festus pronounced the prescribed response: "You have appealed to Caesar. To Caesar you will go!" (25:12). It was a long jealously guarded right of Roman citizens.

Probably Paul had a sense of relief after sitting on "dead center" for two long years. No doubt he was exhilarated to realize he would see Rome at last—Rome, where he longed to preach about Jesus Christ.

Luke tells us, "A few days later King Agrippa and Bernice arrived at Caesarea to pay their respects to Festus" (25:13). Agrippa was Herod Agrippa II, son of Herod Agrippa I who, 16 years before, had commited blasphemy and had been smitten with worms, dying tragically (chap. 12). Herod Agrippa II was the brother of Drusilla, wife of Felix. Only 17 years old when his father died dramatically in A.D. 44, Agrippa was too young, so his father's kingdom was given to someone else.

However, Emperor Claudius, friend of the family, gave a small kingdom to Agrippa in A.D. 50. As a puppet king of Rome, Agrippa ruled a territory including Galilee and Peraea.

As secular head over the Jewish religion, he appointed the high priests and dabbled in the affairs of the Temple. But Agrippa didn't allow his religious knowledge and responsibilities to interfere with his pursuit of pleasure and immorality. Agrippa outraged the Jews by committing incest with his own sister, Bernice. She had had two previous marriages. Later, Bernice became mistress to Roman Emperors Vespasian and Titus.

Coming to his Roman superior, Agrippa could explain the curious things about the Jews over whom Festus had come to rule. They were well known for their excitability and extraordinary stubbornness, a people hard to govern and difficult to understand. Being part Jew and head of Jewish religious affairs, perhaps Agrippa could clear up some things for Festus.

The strange case of Paul came up in their conversation. Agrippa said, "I would like to hear this man myself" (25:22). So it was arranged the next day. "Agrippa and Bernice came with great pomp and entered the audience room with the high ranking officers and the leading men of the city" (25:23).

Paul was brought with his chains. Festus explained that Paul, obviously innocent, had appealed to Caesar. He said to Agrippa, "Therefore I have brought him before all of you, and especially before you, King Agrippa, so that as a result of this investigation I may have something to write. For I think it is unreasonable to send on a prisoner without specifying the charges against him" (25:26-27).

At that point, Agrippa gave Paul permission to speak. Though not legally obligated to attend or to speak, Paul took the opportunity to tell about Jesus Christ. By his powerful message, Paul introduced Agrippa to the Christ of the Crossroads!

Agrippa Heard Christ Presented (Acts 26:1-23)

Paul's defense is the last major sermon recorded in the Book of Acts. The dramatic moment came with Agrippa entering in kingly array and Paul entering in chains. Making no attempt to justify himself, Paul preached about his conversion, the resurrection of Jesus, and Christ's call to serve. The Lord told His followers: "On my account you will be brought before governors and kings as witnesses to them and to the Gentiles. But when they arrest you, do not worry about what to say or how to say it. At that time you will be given what to say, for it will not be you speaking, but the Spirit of your Father speaking through you" (Matt. 10:18-20).

First, Paul presented Christ as the fulfillment of God's promise: "And now it is because of my hope in what God has promised our fathers that I am on trial today. This is the promise our twelve tribes are hoping to see fulfilled as they earnestly serve God day and night. . . . Why should any of you consider it incredible that God raises the dead?" (26:6-8).

Just as God had been faithful to His people in the past, so He would keep His promise of a Savior. Jesus was no accident of history! He was and is God's only begotten Son. God sent Him to take away the sin of the world. "While we were still sinners, Christ died for us" (Rom. 5:8). Writing to the Romans, Paul rejoiced, "What, then, shall we say in response to this? If God is for us, who can be against us? . . . Christ Jesus, who died—more than that, who was raised to life—is at the right hand of God and is also interceding for us" (Rom. 8:31, 34).

Second, Paul presented Christ by personal testimony. He told how the Lord met him on the Damascus Road and changed his life. The dramatic confrontation with Christ could never be dismissed or forgotten. Paul would never be the same having experienced the grace of God.

Though ashamed of what he had been and had done before meeting Jesus, Paul was not ashamed even in chains. He could write, "I am not ashamed of the gospel, because it is the power of God for the salvation of everyone who believes" (Rom. 1:16).

Brownlow North was an evangelist. In his early days he had lived a life of reproach, but God changed him. One day, moments before entering the pulpit to preach, he received a letter. The anonymous author threatened to expose him by producing evidence of his earlier disgrace. The writer said he would interrupt the public service and tell about that sin if North would begin to preach that day.

North took the letter and climbed up the steps to the pulpit. He read the letter aloud to the congregation and admitted that the accusation was true. Confessing all, he testified how Jesus had forgiven him and changed him, and that Christ wanted to do the same for them.

The evidence of his shame was turned to the glory of Christ! That's what forgiveness is all about.

Third, Paul presented Christ as One who had called him to preach: "I am sending you to them to open their eyes and turn them from darkness to light, and from the power of Satan to God, so that they may receive forgiveness of sins and a place among those who are sanctified by faith in me" (26:17-18). Paul was appointed to be an instrument of God's love and mercy to bring people to the Christ of the Crossroads. He had suffered at the hands of Gentiles for being a Jew and suffered at the hands of Jews for preaching to Gentiles. But Jesus had called him to tell the good news of God's love.

A missionary to India said his friends in America thought he was a fool for going to India, and the Indians thought he was a fool for coming.[2]

Standing before Agrippa, Paul said, "I was not disobedient to the vision from heaven. . . . I preached that they should repent and turn to God and prove their repentance by their deeds. . . . But I have had God's help to this very day, and so I stand here and testify to small and great alike. I am saying nothing beyond what the prophets and Moses said would happen—that the Christ would suffer and, as the first to rise from the dead, would proclaim light to his own people and to the Gentiles" (26:19-20, 22-23).

William Barker illustrated: "Martin Niemoller, the German Christian arrested by the Nazis and subjected to nearly nine years of prison horrors, made a speaking tour of American churches shortly after World War II. Two newspaper reporters were overheard discussing Niemoller's address in one city. 'Imagine!' muttered one reporter disgustedly. 'Nine years in a Nazi prison and all he can talk about is Jesus Christ!'

"Two years in a Caesarean cell and all Paul could talk about was Jesus Christ! He did not sensationalize his experiences; he did not protest his innocence. In the third, final, and most complete presentation of Paul's conversion experience in Acts, Paul testified about *the* King to *a* king. Not particularly concerned about his future or his rights or his safety, Paul was most anxious to proclaim Jesus Christ."[3]

Agrippa heard Christ faithfully and powerfully proclaimed.

Agrippa Felt Christ Probing (Acts 26:24-27)

As Agrippa was brought to the Christ of the Crossroads, he and Festus felt the impact of the Holy Spirit. They had been challenged to hear God's Word and to turn to God for help. Each was conscious of his own sins. God has promised to honor the preaching of His Word with the probing of the Holy Spirit. Men can present God's truth, but only God's Spirit can convict of sin. The Holy Spirit pricks the spiritual heart until a person realizes his need for God's help and love. Then one knows he must change. For, if he sins, he does not just break God's law; he breaks God's heart!

Festus didn't know how to handle the message of Christ, nor did he understand the inner conviction. Suddenly he blurted out, "You are out of your mind, Paul! . . . Your great learning is driving you insane" (26:24). He thought Paul insane because Jesus mattered so much to him, more than life itself! Festus got strangely uncomfortable in the presence of the Holy Spirit. He was like many people today who "think of Christianity in terms of living a good life, helping others, giving to the Red Cross, and even attending church occasionally. But [when] you talk . . . about personal devotion to Jesus . . . or [yielding] to the Holy Spirit, or the Second Coming of our Lord, or future judgment, they . . . get restless, examine their watches, and suddenly remember an appointment somewhere else."[4]

"'I am not insane, most excellent Festus,' Paul replied. 'What I am saying is true and reasonable. The king is familiar with these things . . . I am convinced that none of this has escaped his notice, because it was not done in a corner'" (26:25-26). Agrippa had some knowledge of the Scriptures. But there's danger in superficial familiarity with Christian truth. Many people have had a lifelong familiarity with Jesus and know much about Him. Tragically, they don't know Jesus personally.

You may know all the books of the Bible, be able to quote verses, know the familiar terminology, and have a conversant knowledge of Bible truths, yet still be as lost as an unlearned pagan. The question the Holy Spirit asks is: "What will you do with Jesus?" (cf. Matt. 27:22).

Paul turned to Agrippa, "King Agrippa, do you believe the prophets?" (26:27). He really put Agrippa on the spot. If Agrippa believed the Old Testament prophecies, he had no excuse for ignoring Jesus as Messiah. Jesus' birth, life, death, and resurrection had all been prophesied plainly. But if Agrippa denied belief in the prophets, he would outrage the Jews, of whom he was secular leader. Paul was a master at dilemma!

Before Agrippa could answer, Paul continued, "I know you do" (v. 27). Agrippa believed the Old Testament prophecies; but knowledge alone has no effect. One must trust the character of God. Many people intellectually believe in the Good News, but it makes no moral or spiritual difference in their lives. "Do you believe . . . ? I know you do."

Agrippa knew better but had continued to live in an incestuous relationship with his sister. There's nothing more impotent than a firmly believed but neglected truth!

The Holy Spirit was prodding Agrippa's heart, and Paul knew it. A model sermon, Paul concluded with a direct appeal for a personal decision about Jesus. Christ was beckoning at the crossroads. Agrippa felt the tug of God on his heart. He knew he should come to Christ.

Agrippa Let Christ Pass (Acts 26:28)

With Paul looking him in the eyes and God speaking in his heart, Agrippa responded, "Almost thou persuadest me to be a Christian" (v. 28, KJV).

We would probably have to hear the tone of his voice and see the look on his face before we could be certain if he was being serious or sarcastic. Literally, he says, "In a little you are persuading me to make a Christian." As I studied this retort, there seems to be three interpretations of Agrippa's words. I believe all three represent human need.

First, Agrippa may have spoken a word of derision. "Do you think that in such a short time you can persuade me to be a Christian?" (NIV). "With trivial proofs like these, you expect me to become a Christian?" (TLB). "At this rate, . . . it won't be long before you believe you have made a Christian of me!" (Moffatt). Perhaps from a lack of interest Agrippa is saying, "You've got to be kidding! Me—a Christian?"

Christ stood at the crossroads of Agrippa's life, but Agrippa refused, hiding behind a wisecrack to avoid embarrassment. Maybe there was contempt in the words "Me—a Christian?" Agrippa with his crown could only see Paul with his chains.

However, the Good News is a great leveler; all men stand on the same ground at the Cross. Crowns and chains mean nothing before God. We all need the Savior. We all must confess our own sins. That's humbling to those who think they stand on some real or imagined pedestal. Do you find it difficult to submit yourself to Christ and admit your spiritual poverty?

Second, Agrippa may have spoken a word of skepticism. "In brief you are trying to persuade me and make a Christian of me!" (Williams). "In this short time do you think you will make me a Christian?" (TEV). "You think it will not take much to win me over and make a Christian of me" (NEB). Perhaps from a lack of faith, Agrippa is saying, "It's too good to be true. Impossible!"

Not yet convinced, he makes no room for grace. "It just can't be." Agrippa, like many of us, found it difficult to believe that God freely forgives. "There must be something more, something *I* can do." We try so hard to have a part in earning our salvation. It's so hard to believe that I can do nothing to make God love me more; and I can do nothing to make God love me less.

In 2 Kings 5, Naaman, military leader, got leprosy. Hearing about Elisha, Naaman went to see him. "Elisha sent a messenger to say to him, 'Go, wash yourself seven times in the Jordan, and your flesh will be restored and you will be cleansed.'

"But Naaman went away angry and said, 'I thought that he would surely come out to me and stand and call on the name of the Lord his God, wave his hand over the spot and cure me of my leprosy. . . .' So he turned and went off in a rage. [Naaman wanted to be treated as a *great man* who happened to be a *leper.* Elisha insisted on treating him as a *leper* who happened to be a *great man.]*

"Naaman's servants went to him and said, 'My father, if the prophet had told you to do some great thing, would you not have done it? How much more, then, when he tells you, "Wash and be cleansed"!' So he went down and dipped himself in the Jordan seven times, as the man of God had told him, and his flesh was restored and became clean like that of a young boy" (2 Kings 5:10-14).

In refusing God's free grace, we push away Jesus' atonement at the Cross and brush past the Christ at the crossroads. What He offers as a free gift, we want to earn by self-effort. Like Naaman, we look for some great thing to do, while, instead, God asks us to trust and obey. "Nothing in my hand I bring, / Simply to Thy cross I cling" (Augustus M. Toplady).

A drowning man often gets his arms and legs wrapped frantically around his would-be rescuer and destroys them both. How much better to relax in the arms of the lifeguard and allow him to do his great work.

Can you trust Christ enough to turn loose of everything and let yourself down in His love? Why struggle with your sins when you can just accept His gift of eternal life with pardon, purity, and peace?

King Edward VIII of England was concerned with the slum conditions near the waterfront. The king stopped at a run-down house of a social outcast. Hearing the knock at his door, the man shouted gruffly, "Who is it?"

The answer came, "I am your king. May I come in?"

Thinking it a cruel joke, the man refused to open the door. Since a man's house is his castle, the king would not force his way in. He walked away from the locked door.

The King of Kings comes at least once to each of us, saying, "Behold, I stand at the door, and knock: if any man hear my voice, and open the door, I will come in to him, and will sup with him, and he with me" (Rev. 3:20, KJV). How tragic to miss opening that door!

Third, Agrippa may have spoken a word of conviction. "Almost thou persuadest me to be a Christian" (KJV). "In a short time you will persuade me to become a Christian" (NASB). "Much more of this . . . and you will be making me a Christian!" (Phillips). Perhaps from a lack of decision, Agrippa is saying, "How I wish I could! If only . . . !"

Agrippa experienced the force of Paul's persuasive arguments and felt the prodding of Christ, but he tried to conceal his deep feelings with jest. Spiritually shaken, he may have been embarrassed in the presence of Festus and Bernice. For an instant he halted, close to a decision: "Almost thou persuadest me to be a Christian."

The barrier of prejudice halted him. Look at Paul's chains; Christians seem bound up and have such a limited life! What a wrong idea of a Christian! Paul's spirit soared, while Agrippa was chained to sin.

The barrier of people halted him. He was afraid Festus would think him mad also. The cry of the crowd and the howl of the herd stopped him in his tracks. Yes, you can let your friends laugh you into hell, but they can't laugh you out of it!

The barrier of pleasure halted him. He had sold himself to pleasure. He knew he couldn't keep Bernice and continue in sinful pleasure and be right with God. The Bible says Moses "chose to be mistreated along with the people of God rather than to enjoy the pleasures of sin for a short time" (Heb. 11:25).

The barrier of partial persuasion halted Agrippa. "Almost" is not good enough. He was pulled, but not fully persuaded. It takes 100 percent to be a Christian. Agrippa's story is near achievement and total loss. "Almost" is to utterly fail. God's peace and pardon were within reach. God's hand of mercy beckoned; but "almost persuaded," Agrippa chose for time and eternity to remain without God. To be "almost persuaded" is to be altogether lost.

The Christ of the Crossroads had touched his heart, but Agrippa withdrew from this strange and unexpected power. It was his hour of grace, but he withdrew, leaving Jesus behind him.

Paul answered, "I pray God that not only you but all who are listening to me today may become what I am, except for these chains" (26:29).

It was getting too hot for Agrippa! He closed the interview and stood up with his friends: "They left the room, and while talking with one another, they said, 'This man is not doing anything that deserves death or imprisonment.' Agrippa said to Festus, 'This man could have been set free if he had not appealed to Caesar'" (26:31-32).

Let me give you a free translation that fits our day: "They left the sanctuary, and while talking with one another, they said, 'This man preached a nice sermon.'" Little did they realize what a fateful moment they had just passed through. They let Jesus pass by. The Christ of the Crossroads was not on trial; they were. "Almost thou persuadest me to be a Christian"—almost but lost!

Whittier told of a farm girl working in the fields. She felt great pangs of disappointment when she saw the distinguished man riding by, for she remembered how near she came to marrying him. She speaks these lines:

For of all sad words of tongue or pen,
The saddest are these: "It might have been!"

This same sad story could be told over and over again by those once "almost persuaded." Fearing public opinion, criticism, ridicule, loss of friends or social standing, they wait for some more convenient time. But the time to do business with God is when His Spirit calls to your heart. The Bible warns, "Do not boast about tomorrow, for you do not know what a day may bring forth" (Prov. 27:1). If you leave unmelted and unbelieving, you may be adding one more stone to the barrier you are building to shut you out from holiness and happiness, from hope and heaven. The decisive question is again, "What will you do with Jesus?"

Christ stands at the crossroads. Don't let Him pass by. Fall at His feet and receive His forgiveness and love. If Jesus physically stood here at this crossroads, what would He say? Would He tell us what miserable sinners we are? No! He would begin telling us what great people we can become if we will only let His Spirit of faith, hope, and love fill every part of our lives.

Christ awaits at the crossroads of your heart. You have heard Christ presented. If you have felt Christ probing, don't let Christ pass by. Pray this simple prayer:

Pass me not, O gentle Saviour;
Hear my humble cry.
While on others Thou art calling,
Do not pass me by.

—Fanny J. Crosby

8

When Life Goes to Pieces

Acts 27:1-44

Exercising his citizen's right to appeal to Caesar, Paul soon was sailing toward Rome, the imperial city—a 1,700-mile voyage from Israel. Never again would Paul see the Holy City of his fathers. As the coastline faded away, the scene of Christian history shifted with Paul to Rome.

Luke's following narrative is so vivid and precise that maritime scholars claim it to be the most accurate account of seamanship in that era of history. The eyewitness descriptions of storm and shipwreck are the most vivid of any contemporary literature.

Under the command of Julius, Roman centurion, Paul and other prisoners put out to sea and landed in Sidon the next day. During the layover, Julius let Paul and his company "go to his friends so they might provide for his needs" (v. 3). The Greek word for "provide for," a medical term for taking care of a sick man, suggests Paul was ill.

Westerly winds forced the ship north around Cyprus to dock in Myra, regular port of call for grain ships sailing between Egypt and Rome.

An early Christian bishop of Myra has become famous: St. Nicholas, patron saint of children and known in America today as Santa Claus. Once Nicholas sailed on a pilgrimage to Israel. In a dream during the voyage, he felt warned that a storm was brewing. Telling the ship's crew, Nicholas assured them that God would protect; they need not fear. When the storm struck and the ship went out of control, Nicholas prayed. Soon the wind slackened. As a result, St. Nicholas became patron saint of sailors.

In Myra, Julius transferred his prisoners to an Egyptian grain ship headed for Rome. Usually the ships were 140 feet long with a beam (width) of 36 feet and a draft (depth) of 33 feet. Two hundred and seventy-six people were on the ship's roster. Big and bulky, the old Mediterranean ships were unable to sail upwind very steeply. Luke noted, "We made slow headway for many days" (v. 7). Head winds forced them to change course and go on the leeward (downwind) side of Crete, an island 140 miles long and 35 miles wide, equidistant from Europe, Asia, and Africa. Crete was the ancient home of the Phoenicians, known in Old Testament times as Philistines who invaded Canaan. Those maritime invaders gave to Canaan their name Philistia or Palestine.

Paul's ship arrived in Fair Havens. Luke says, "Much time had been lost, and sailing had already become dangerous because by now it was after the Fast" (v. 9). From mid-September until early November, sailing was risky in the Mediterranean Sea. And from November 11 until early March, all sailing stopped. "The Fast"—Yom Kippur—celebrated the Jewish Day of Atonement, their New Year's Day. Food is avoided as a means to afflict the soul and stimulate prayer. The ram's horn—the shofar—is blown on Yom Kippur, most holy day of the Jewish calendar. Since Yom Kippur had passed, it was by then possibly late October, the risky season for sailing.

"So Paul warned them, 'Men, I can see that our voyage is going to be disastrous and bring great loss to ship and cargo, and to our own lives also'" (vv. 9-10). With three shipwrecks in his past experience, Paul knew the dangers of the season (2 Cor. 11:25). He did what he could to avoid danger and to change the course of action, but no one would listen. Officers overruled, deciding to sail on to Phoenix and spend the winter. Majority vote only decides what people think, not necessarily what is right.

"When a gentle south wind began to blow, they thought they had obtained what they wanted; so they weighed anchor and sailed along the shore of Crete" (v. 13). The captain and officers, like people today, erroneously believed that because a gentle breeze blows today, it will always be that way.

Luke's words, "Before very long" (v. 14), hint that things don't always stay calm and easy and uncomplicated; there's more to come! In the unexpected storm, we get a glimpse of the men wrapping cables and lines around the hull of the ship, attempting to hold everything together. There are times when life goes to pieces. What then? God never promised an easy voyage free from storm and shipwreck in life. But God's Word assures us that the Lord himself will stand by in times of panic, when life goes to pieces.

One man lamented, "Life for me has gone to pieces!" Many wonderful years and rich blessings had come to his journey. He seemed to get all the good breaks, and the sun always seemed to shine on him. But suddenly storms came! Everything seemed to come loose. Life just went to pieces. Many people have experienced the same thing in life. If that should happen to you, what can you count on?

When Life Goes to Pieces, You Can Count On God's Presence (vv. 13-26)

Unseen by frantic passengers and crew, Paul says, "Last night an angel of the God whose I am and whom I serve stood beside me" (v. 23).

God is there!

God is there in moments of confusion. Paul and his company enjoyed the "gentle south wind"—serene, undisturbed tranquility of spirit. Some people think the converted person is always borne along by balmy breezes of outward peace. "Before very long, a wind of hurricane force" (v. 14). Temptation, heaviness of spirit, doubt, persecution, or sorrow can rock your boat. If that's not enough, Luke adds, "We took . . . a violent battering from the storm" (v. 18). At times, you may wonder, "Can this really be happening to me? What in the world is going on?" But the Lord himself is standing by.

God is there in moments of anxiety. "The ship was caught by the storm . . . so we gave way to it and were driven along" (v. 15). They were out of control, being driven where they didn't want to go. The trailing lifeboat got shoved up against the stern, so they hauled it in. The huge mast, whipping in the pitching seas and turbulent winds, acted like a lever, prying the ship's planks apart. Cables called "undergirders" were passed around the hull under the keel and winched tight, trying to hold the ship together. Crew and passengers strained in a mighty human effort to bind the hull against the force of the storm. It was only a matter of time before the pressures would erupt into pieces.

What a description of anxiety—a word meaning "pulled in two directions." But the Lord himself is standing near.

God is there in moments of loss. "We took such a violent battering from the storm that the next day they began to throw the cargo overboard" (v. 18). Things they thought they couldn't do without were thrown aside to save their lives! Trinkets and treasures thought to be so important were tossed away. When life goes to pieces, it's surprising how little we really need!

God is there in moments of desperation. "On the third day, they threw the ship's tackle overboard with their own hands" (v. 19). We aren't ready for the ministry God has given to us until we start letting loose of pride, self-centeredness, temper, and unholy attitudes. In the storm, with life hanging in the balance, we find out what must be disposed of! When life goes to pieces, God forces us to lighten our cargo—all the stuff we drag along to drag us down. "Let us throw off everything that hinders and the sin that so easily entangles" (Heb. 12:1). Even then the Lord himself stands by.

God is there in moments of hopelessness. "When neither sun nor stars appeared for many days and the storm continued raging, we finally gave up all hope of being saved" (v. 20). Unable to get a fix on the sun or stars, the navigators had no idea of their position. They were helplessly lost.

And the Christian doesn't always sail under a cloudless sky and the bright sunlight of glory. When the sun doesn't shine and you feel hopeless, remember two things. First, the sun shines above the clouds. Second, since God is in control, you are still en route to His destination. You are as much on the way to heaven under pressure, temptation, testing, and devoid of exuberance as when the sun shines bright and you are filled with joy. Faith reaches beyond circumstances and finds that the Lord himself stands by. "For there stood by me this night the angel of God, whose I am, and whom I serve, saying, Fear not, Paul; thou must be brought before Caesar: and, lo, God hath given thee all them that sail with thee" (vv. 23-24, KJV).

God speaks!

God speaks a word of faith: "Do not be afraid" (v. 24). When human hope is gone, God has a word of encouragement. Even Paul experienced fear, but God's voice restored hope. Paul could turn to the others and say, "Keep up your courage" (v. 25), "Be of good cheer" (KJV). It's from the word for "singing."

A husband kept vigil beside his dying wife's bed, watching the pain etched in her face. Overcome by doubts and fears, he said to her with bitterness, "How can you accept this so patiently? How can you hold on to your sense of humor? How can you keep an unquestioning faith in God?"

She nodded toward the window. Outside, a mockingbird perched on the railing, singing his heart out. "There," she said, "that's my answer. If you look close, that little bird has only one leg. I've watched it struggling day after day to keep its balance. I've seen it digging for food, fighting for survival, trying to rest occasionally. But that bird has never quit its happy song. I think God sent it to me for a reminder of my dependence upon the Lord. If He will take care of His creatures, how much more will He do for His children!"

God speaks a word of destiny: "Thou must be brought before Caesar" (v. 24, KJV). The Lord had a job for Paul. God's assignment was bigger than surviving a storm: He planned for him to preach Christ in the capital city of the empire! A sense of destiny gave Paul great confidence.

God speaks a word of peace: "God has graciously given you the lives of all who sail with you" (v. 24). These 275 other people on board would sense Paul's trust in God. Any of us would like the assurance that our circle will be unbroken!

God inspires!

When life goes to pieces, you can count on God's presence. Paul responded, "Wherefore, sirs, be of good cheer: for I believe God" (v. 25, KJV). He did *not* say, "I believe *in* God!" At that point, many on board probably believed in God. Most people believe in God, but it doesn't make much difference in their lives.

A frightened passenger asked the captain during a storm, "Sir, are we in danger?"

The captain answered, "No, ma'am. The sailors are still swearing. Don't need to worry until they start praying."

One old seaman got caught in a storm that threatened to sink the ship. All were filled with fear. Someone asked, "Does anyone here know how to pray? Please, will someone pray?"

Trembling with anxiety, the old seaman said, "I don't know how, but I'll try." He began, "Dear God, I haven't asked You for anything in over 15 years. And if You will save us from this storm, I promise not to bother You again for another 15!"

Paul testified, "I believe God" (KJV); "I have faith in God" (NIV). That kind of faith trusts God in the face of disappointments, disasters, and disillusionments. Believing God means you can relax and settle back with complete confidence in God's everlasting arms of love. Paul believed God because he had learned to listen to God's voice. The lamp of hope burned in Paul's heart. He trusted in "the God whose I am and whom I serve" (v. 23). Those frightened men had missed the truth, "You are not your own; you were bought at a price" (1 Cor. 6:19-20). You belong to the Lord, and He belongs to you!

Faith in God makes a difference. In 1735 John Wesley was crossing the Atlantic Ocean when his ship got hit by a storm. Wesley wrote in his diary that he felt "unwilling to die." Twenty-six Moravians on board expressed no fear or worry. Curious, Wesley asked, "Weren't you afraid?"

A Moravian man replied, "I thank God, no."

"And your women and children—were they afraid?"

The man answered, "Our women and children are not afraid to die either."

Their quiet confidence in God was used by the Lord to later bring John Wesley to a personal trust in God. The Bible says, "We have this hope as an anchor for the soul, firm and secure" (Heb. 6:19). What can you count on?

When Life Goes to Pieces, You Can Count On God's Providence (vv. 27-38)

For 14 days and nights the ship was driven by the storm. They had a lot of time to think—and wait! God wasn't finished with them yet. Waiting in suspense and idleness can breed despair.

While waiting, accept God's detours. Paul and his men could not sit down and read Acts 28 to see why God wanted them in a certain place at this time. But you can trust God's providence, even when it doesn't make sense.

A Sunday School teacher told the story of Abraham preparing to sacrifice his son, Isaac. When it got rather vivid, a little girl interrupted: "Please don't go on. That's a terrible story!"

Another girl spoke up, "It'll be all right, Cheryl. This is one of God's stories, and all God's stories come out all right!"

God's detours will turn out all right, also. Learn to trust Him!

While waiting, do what you can. Four hundred and eighty miles after passing Cauda, their last sight of land, "about midnight the sailors sensed they were approaching land. They took soundings and found that the water was a hundred and twenty feet deep. A short time later they took soundings again and found it was ninety feet deep. Fearing that we would be dashed against the rocks, they dropped four anchors from the stern" (vv. 27-29). Those men did everything right they knew to do. Waiting on God's providence should include our best judgment and our best efforts.

While waiting, pray. "They dropped four anchors . . . and prayed for daylight" (v. 29). When you've done all you can, claim God's promises and pray for His dawn to break! Man's extremity is God's opportunity. As we pray, we find God's hand of deliverance reaching out to us.

William A. Tolbert wrote, "When Major Allen Lindberg was pilot of a Flying Fortress forced down at sea while on his way to Australia, he and his crew of nine men were given up for lost.

"'We just had time to shove off on two rubber rafts, without a crumb of food or a drop of water,' Major Lindberg reported. 'The boys were pretty worried—all except Sergeant Albert Hernandez of Dallas, our tail gunner. Right away that lad started praying, and pretty soon he startled us by announcing that he knew God had heard him and would help us out.'

"Drifting beneath a broiling sun with lips too cracked and tongues too swollen to join Hernandez in singing hymns, the men continued praying just the same. Three days later, just before nightfall, they saw the outline of a small island and soon after that the unbelievable spectacle of three canoes filled with naked men coming toward them. Their rescuers turned out to be Australian aborigines—black-skinned, kinky-headed fishermen from the mainland several hundred miles away. They told Lindberg that the day before they had been homeward bound with their catch, when a strange urge impelled them to change their course, and steer for this uninhabited and worthless bit of coral. And from the atoll they had spied Lindberg and his companions."[1]

Don't sit with blank eyes waiting for something to happen. Pray! Talk to God who hears and answers prayer. Tell Him about your situation, for He cares for you.

While waiting, maintain fellowship with people of faith. "In an attempt to escape from the ship, the sailors let the lifeboat down into the sea, pretending they were going to lower some anchors from the bow. Then Paul said to the centurion and the soldiers, 'Unless these men stay with the ship, you cannot be saved.' So the soldiers cut the ropes that held the lifeboat and let it fall away" (vv. 30-32).

When life goes to pieces, don't run out on God's people. Paul knew God had decreed they would arrive safely, but Paul took precautions to keep the skills of the sailors where God could use them. There's always danger in splintering the bond of fellowship. God would rescue them altogether. So, keep close to God's family. The Bible says, "Bear ye one another's burdens, and so fulfil the law of Christ" (Gal. 6:2, KJV).

While waiting, seek nourishment for strength. "Just before dawn Paul urged them all to eat. '. . . You need it to survive.' . . . he took some bread and gave thanks to God in front of them all. Then he broke it and began to eat. They were all encouraged and ate some food themselves" (vv. 33-36). Like the father of a Hebrew family, Paul thanked God for the meal. What a heartfelt prayer of thanksgiving! The strength of nourishment and the attitude of confidence broke the spell of depression: "Then were they all of good cheer" (v. 36, KJV). God used Paul to bring them out of despair.

When life goes to pieces, don't quit! Seek spiritual and emotional nourishment from God's Word and from the fellowship of God's family. What can you count on?

When Life Goes to Pieces, You Can Count On God's Protection (vv. 39-44)

The storm ended in shipwreck, but God saved them out of it.

Recognize God's provision. "When daylight came, they did not recognize the land, but they saw a bay with a sandy beach, where they decided to run the ship aground if they could" (v. 39). God brought them to the precise spot where He wanted them. On the northeast shore of the island of Malta, just 62 miles south of Sicily! To those sailors, that sandy beach looked like a wide-open door. They thought, How lucky can you get? But God had provided for them. What an echo from the Psalms:

> Others went out on the sea in ships; . . .
> . . . the Lord . . . spoke and stirred up a tempest
> that lifted high the waves. . . .
> in their peril their courage melted away.
> They reeled and staggered like drunken men; . . .
> Then they cried out to the Lord in their trouble,
> and he brought them out of their distress. . . .
> and he guided them to their desired haven.
> *(Ps. 107:23-28, 30)*

Respond to God's opportunities. Seeing God's provision, the men acted at once. Don't let God's opportunities slip by! "Cutting loose the anchors, they left them in the sea" (v. 40). If you don't understand sailing craft, that means they were committed to action. There's no turning back; it's straight ahead. "Then they hoisted the foresail to the wind and made for the beach" (v. 40). With all the power available, they sailed right for God's haven. And if problems have piled high in your life, just watch for God's opportunities and seize them. It's not always easy or comfortable, but it's just right.

Release to God's care. When you've done your best, leave all behind. Paul's ship hit the sandbar and broke to pieces. There wasn't a thing worth going after. Turn loose, hands down, and leave all behind, trusting yourself to God's care.

When life goes to pieces, look around. Those fellows grabbed planks and boards and pieces of the ship and "everyone reached land in safety" (v. 44). Many a person's faith has been built after life has been broken. Jesus Christ came to save broken lives.

Trust God's care and leap forward. At some point, there is always the leap of faith. Pick up the pieces and go on! Take the broken pieces of your hopes and dreams and goals, and go to shore. God guides and protects to the last breaking wave. God stood by through it all, from beginning to end. God can take the broken pieces and make something beautiful and good. The Lord himself stands by and calls out, "Fear not, for I have redeemed you; I have summoned you by name; you are mine. When you pass through the waters, I will be with you" (Isa. 43:1-2). Your God has called you by name. In life's worst storms, He is standing by.

George and Donna Rench, missionaries to Indonesia, got caught in a massive riot in Jakarta. Unaware of the danger until it was too late, their car was surrounded by rioters, police, tanks, and fire trucks. Columns of black smoke rolled around them as they eased their car through the streets, dodging debris. Overturned cars had been set on fire, and foreign-made motorcycles were thrown into a river.

Donna wrote, "Seeing the angry rioters still very close to us we considered leaving the car and running to safety. Yet the Lord seemed to check George . . . and we stayed inside the car.

"Then George remembered the tape from Pasadena First Church. Hoping to relieve the tension, he inserted the cassette into the player and we . . . heard Rev. [Earl] Lee say: 'I have never been so aware of the leading of the Holy Spirit as I have been [this year]. In the little, little details of life, Jesus has led me all the way.'

". . . We knew beyond the shadow of a doubt that God had led us to Indonesia. . . . We were in His hands. . . . God was giving George wisdom as he drove . . . choosing the right streets . . . sometimes down one-way roads the wrong way.

". . . George and I were both praying as we sensed the tenseness everywhere. Fear had crept into the car and was riding in the front seat with us. . . .

"Suddenly a car loaded with yelling rioters careened toward us. We were terrified. . . . Almost aloud George agonized: *Why have I come to Indonesia?*

"Then the gentle voice of the Holy Spirit said: 'George, remember you have not come here by your own choice but by Mine. I brought you here.' . . . The crowds were all around us, and the unreasonable violence could erupt again at any moment. How we prayed! We were so vulnerable.

"Our ears picked up from the cassette words which continued to penetrate our fears. . . . No one will ever be able to tell us that what was taped in Pasadena, Calif., on December 30 was not meant for us on January 15 . . . halfway around the world. The choir was singing . . .

When I met with storm and trials, and my heart was filled with fear;
When there was no one around to speak a word of help and cheer;
When I met defeat and failure, and my courage ebbed away,
When it seemed my life was useless, and I found it hard to pray;
Then the Lord himself stood by me, and I had no cause to fear;
Yes, the Lord himself stood by me! All was changed, fully changed;
All was changed, sweetly changed; all was changed when He drew near.

"Then the chorus of that inspired song . . . filled our car again:

Then the Lord himself stood by me . . .
All was changed, fully changed . . .
*Sweetly changed when He drew near.**

"Peace flooded the car and our inmost souls. We know the Lord was with us. We felt His presence clearly. He was in the car guiding and helping us through the riot. The fear *was* gone . . . the Lord *himself* was there sitting between us . . . *there were three in the front seat*—Jesus, George, and I."[2]

Even when life goes to pieces, the Lord himself stands by, saying, "Do not be afraid!" Make Him Captain of your life. It's better to face the stormy waters with Christ than smooth waters without Him!

*John W. Peterson, "The Lord Stood by Me." © Copyright 1972 by Singspiration Inc. All rights reserved. Used by permission.

9

Jesus Led Me All the Way

Acts 28:1-31

As the ship was sinking fast, the captain called out, "Anyone here know how to pray?"

One man stepped forward. "I do, sir."

"Good," said the captain. "You pray. The rest of us will put on life jackets. We're one short!"

In Acts 27, the crew and passengers found a man who knew how to pray: the apostle Paul. And they were glad he did: "In this way everyone reached land in safety" (27:44). Luke continues the story, "Once safely on shore, we found out that the island was called Malta" (28:1). Ancient Phoenicians had inhabited the island 10 centuries before Christ and called it Melita, meaning in their Punic language, "Land of Refuge." A strategic spot during World War II, Malta suffered from more than 1,200 bombing attacks.

Luke noted, "The islanders showed us unusual kindness" (v. 2). Very likely the men salvaged shipwrecks, living off the misfortunes of careless navigators along one of the world's busiest maritime lanes.

In Jutland, Denmark, salvors still follow their old code of ethics: "The safety of shipwrecked crews always came first, and salvage second. Every Sunday in church the islanders would offer the traditional prayer of salvors the world over: 'O Lord, protect all sailors upon the sea—but if they must founder, Lord, let it happen here.'"[1]

In kindness, the salvors gave assistance: "They built a fire and welcomed us all because it was raining and cold" (v. 2). That's good, practical help. Today there's too much indifference that says, "'Go, I wish you well; keep warm and well fed,' but does nothing about his physical needs"; and the rhetorical question follows: "what good is it?" (James 2:16).

With 276 survivors, there was much to do: "Paul gathered a pile of brushwood and, as he put it on the fire, a viper, driven out by the heat, fastened itself on his hand. When the islanders saw the snake hanging from his hand, they said to each other, 'This man must be a murderer; for though he escaped from the sea, Justice has not allowed him to live.' But Paul shook the snake off into the fire and suffered no ill effects. The people expected him to swell up or suddenly fall dead, but after waiting a long time and seeing nothing unusual happen to him, they changed their minds and said he was a god" (vv. 3-6).

Those islanders expressed the basic idea of natural religion: retribution. It underlies all forms of mythologies and religions: Justice will get you in the end. That's the first instinct of religion. Surely the guilty man's sword will fail in a duel. Followed to its logical conclusion, the idea becomes the rationale for war: "Might makes right." Sadly, many Christians have gotten not much farther along in their spiritual pilgrimmage than the "sin now, pay later" syndrome. Real Christianity soars far beyond that desert plain of religion. Justice gives you what you deserve. Mercy doesn't give you what you deserve. Grace gives you what you don't deserve! Through Jesus Christ, "grace" is "good news."

Experience shows that the criminal can sleep as soundly as a baby, that the storm at sea can wreck a Christian's boat, that a good man can get snakebit while doing good. The Book of Job deals with the age-old question, "Is evil the result of personal sin?" Natural man ranks crime above sin, but the good news of Jesus corrects both.

Ancient Greek myths represent the gods as having power over snakes. So, when the islanders saw Paul shake off the snake into the fire and survive, "they changed their minds and said he was a god." Sometimes unexpected troubles hinder our service for the Lord. Do what Paul did: Shake them off. Don't allow Satan's roadblocks to paralyze you! Shake them off. God has a purpose for your life, and nothing can prevent that if you will shake off the blows and keep trusting Jesus Christ for guidance and strength.

As Paul reaches the last leg of his long-awaited journey to Rome, one can see how the Lord led him each step of the way. Looking back, Luke could see God's hand in the affairs of the Church and of Paul the missionary.

John Wesley White told of a university football player who committed his life to Christ one night during a crusade. The athlete explained, "I got tired of playing the game of life without being able to see the goalposts!"

Paul never lost sight of the goalposts. He knew Jesus had led him all the way. Even from his prison cell, Paul wrote, "But this one thing I do, forgetting those things which are behind, and reaching forth unto those things which are before, I press toward the mark for the prize of the high calling of God in Christ Jesus" (Phil. 3:13-14, KJV).

On this last lap in the Book of Acts, we'll see how Jesus led.

Jesus Leads to Human Need (vv. 7-9)

"There was an estate nearby that belonged to Publius, the chief official of the island. He welcomed us to his home and for three days entertained us hospitably. His father was sick in bed, suffering from fever and dysentery. Paul went in to see him and, after prayer, placed his hands on him and healed him. When this had happened, the rest of the sick on the island came and were cured" (vv. 7-9).

Paul may have heard of Malta, but he didn't plan to go there. Yet on that island was great human need: many sick, suffering, needy people. Who can imagine the desperate prayers that arose from family and friends of the sick and suffering? Wherever disease and death and sorrow lurk, hearts are broken. But no apostles had planned to go to that island. Little did Paul realize what God was doing. In order to get Paul to that island of need, He sent a storm that drove Paul within swimming distance of the beach!

John Oster said, "Thank God that He knows wherever an island of need exists. He knows where our island is. He knows every pocket of poverty, every place of need in this world. He knows every nation, every state, every family, every situation. His eye is upon suffering humanity. I thank Him for it! . . .

"God wants us to reach the needy people of this world. But most of us will never go until God sends a storm! It may be a financial storm, a marital storm, or a spiritual storm. (And maybe even an ecclesiastical storm!) In the great upheavals of life, we must not complain. If we stay sweet, trust in Jesus and lean upon God—even when we think our life is ruined—God can use contrary winds to drive us into an area of ministry that we never dreamed could be ours."[2]

At Malta, Paul and Luke were the first medical missionary team. Two different Greek words describe what happened: First, "Paul . . . after prayer, placed his hands on him and healed him" (v. 8). This word for "healed" conveys the idea of healing as a completed act, "wholeness" immediately. Second, "the rest of the sick on the island came and were cured" (v. 9). The word for "cured"—from *therapeuō*—conveys the idea of the healing process from its beginning. It suggests "to treat medically." It was not prayer only nor medicine only, but both. Paul and Luke, pastor and physician, worked together under God as a healing team. God used them to meet great human need. The Bible is the greatest book on wholeness and well-being ever written, God's *Owner's Handbook Manual* from the Builder himself!

Jesus Leads to a Ready-made Fellowship (vv. 10-15)

Luke wrote in his diary, "They honored us in many ways and when we were ready to sail, they furnished us with the supplies we needed. After three months we put out to sea in a ship that had wintered in the island" (vv. 10-11). An early spring opened up the seaways again, and Julius, the centurion, booked them on an Egyptian ship headed for Rome by the name of *Twin Brothers.* The figurehead was a carving of Castor and Pollux, two mythical sons of Jupiter, legendary protectors of navigation. According to Greek and Roman mythology, Castor and Pollux were taken up into the sky and became the two stars in the constellation Gemini.

The grain ship stopped for three days in Syracuse, port-city of Sicily, the largest Mediterranean island. A famous Greek city, Syracuse was founded about 735 B.C.

Next, their ship sailed across the Straits of Messina to Rhegium at the toe of the Italian "boot." It, too, was an ancient city founded by Greek sailors. The next day, on a beautiful south wind, they sailed to Puteoli, passing three famous volcanoes, including Mount Vesuvius, covered with lush green vines. No one dreamed that in only a few years—A.D. 79—it would blow its top, engulfing cities like the wicked Pompeii with a force three times greater than our recent Mount St. Helen's eruption. During that cataclysmic event, thousands of people died, including the wife and son of Felix, former governor of Judea.

Paul and his party disembarked at Puteoli, modern Puzzuoli, on the Bay of Naples, a port-city for Rome. Even though Rome was 141 miles away, excellent roads connected to the capital. Luke wrote, "There we found some brothers who invited us to spend a week with them" (v. 14). In a strange land, Paul and Luke found a brotherhood of Christians reaching out to them as a family. Julius, the centurion, already impressed with these Christians, permitted the group to stay and visit for a week.

Luke continues his account: "And so we came to Rome. The brothers there had heard that we were coming, and they traveled as far as the Forum of Appius and the Three Taverns to meet us" (vv. 14-15). The Forum of Appius was 40 miles from Rome, and Three Taverns was 30 miles from Rome. Paul had written his letter to the Romans three years earlier, so the brothers in Rome were eager to welcome Paul with honor and respect. Word had reached them of Paul's arrival in Italy, so they traveled 30 and 40 miles one way to greet him on the Appian Way, built in 312 B.C.

Can you imagine how Paul felt? "At the sight of these men Paul thanked God and was encouraged" (v. 15). What a beautiful picture of Christian fellowship! "Paul thanked God and was encouraged." Those words imply he had felt anxious and fearful. Perhaps he wondered, Will anyone welcome me? Will I enter Rome as a criminal, escorted only by soldiers? Are Christians in Rome safe? Has the church remained true to the faith, or have Judaizers perverted the Christians from grace into legalism?

But when Paul saw them and felt their love and support, he knew they had the real thing. Christian love has no adequate counterfeit. He could see that the Lord had been preparing the way for him. Not only did he rejoice to find friends, but they were also Jesus' friends and servants. That's the community of fellowship that has no equal.

Notice the progression of encouragement that Paul received. Since he had become captive, three different times Paul received special encouragement. First, in jail, *"the Lord* stood near Paul and said, 'Take courage!'" (23:11). The second time, in the storm, *"an angel* of . . . God . . . stood beside me and said, 'Do not be afraid, Paul'" (27:23-24). This third time, on the road to Rome, anxiety was relieved by *"the brothers,"* fellow Christians living in Rome who came and stood by Paul. God used them to greet Paul in the name of the Lord and to stand by him with good cheer: "At the sight of these men Paul thanked God and was encouraged."

God has a ready-made fellowship for us in the church. These brothers and sisters are His instruments of encouragement and strength made readily available. It's important that we love God whom we cannot see (1 Pet. 1:8); but many times it helps to have someone around with skin on!

Henry Jacobsen noted, "God's people today are often in desperate need of such encouragement. They need to know that in their personal crises there are fellow Christians standing with them. It isn't enough that we pray for one another. We need to *let a troubled brother know how much we care.* These Roman Christians walked 60 or 80 miles so that the apostle would be aware of their love. Are we willing to do the inconvenient thing—to go out of our way as the Roman believers did—to communicate our concern?"[3]

How little it takes sometimes to breed courage in one another. Martin Luther was encouraged and braced to face his enemies at the Diet of Worms by a knight who reached out, patted him on the back, and gave a hearty word of cheer as he passed by. Think of the consequences of that little act of love and encouragement!

Jesus Leads to Divine Appointments (vv. 16-28)

Surely Paul's heartbeat must have sped up as they walked the Appian Way getting closer to Rome. They passed the tall milestones and stately tombs lining both sides of the famous road. Monuments still stand, though in ruins, recording the fame, wealth, and virtues of the dead. Next, Paul would see the beginnings of the Catacombs, where Christians, unwelcome in Jewish cemeteries and unwilling to cremate as Romans, laid their dead. Outside the gates of Rome, Paul would pass the pyramid of Caius Cestius, which still stands. Walking through the Porta Capena, Paul entered Rome at last.

Rome, famous for its roads and scenic boulevards, was built on seven hills along the Tiber River. On the Palatine Hill stood the three houses of Augustus, Tiberius, and Caligula, then joined together as the Palace of the Caesars. Paul would see the splendor of the Temple of Mars, Rome's military god of war. Nearby stood the Forum. Across the way was Circus Maximus, seating 200,000 people, where in the next 100 years or more thousands of Christians would die to satisfy the bloodthirsty appetites of Roman entertainment. The Temple of Saturn was the empire's treasury house. The Temple of Castor and Pollux—Gemini—served as a bureau of weights and measurements for coinage.

However, St. Peter's Basilica, the great architectural wonder, was not there yet. The tourist's favorite—the Colosseum—was not built yet.

Founded in 753 B.C., Rome called herself "mistress of the world." When Paul came, Rome had a population of 1.2 million; half were slaves, and the majority of free men were welfare recipients, enjoying free food and free public entertainment. That financial burden eventually broke the back of the Roman Empire and contributed to its fall.

According to an inscription in Ostia, Rome's seaport, the metropolitan population had reached over 4 million in A.D. 14. Rome was the capital of an empire extending 3,000 miles east and west, 2,000 miles north and south, with a population of 120 million. Geographically, the Roman Empire was as large as the United States of America with half its current population.

After developing Christian centers in Antioch, Philippi, Corinth, Ephesus, and other cities, under God's appointment, Paul would be useful in establishing Christian strategy in Rome, center of the empire. It was no accident. Jesus had led him all the way!

First, Paul had divine appointments with Christians in Rome. Luke wrote, "When we got to Rome, Paul was allowed to live by himself, with a soldier to guard him" (v. 16). Paul was free to receive visitors, even though he did not have liberty himself. The letters he wrote from Rome indicate that many friends and Christians came and went. He strengthened and encouraged those congregations to whom he had written his powerful Roman Epistle.

An old legend tells of a merchant who heard about Paul during his travels around the Mediterranean world. Arriving in Rome on business, he looked up Paul in prison. Timothy arranged for an interview with Paul. After visiting for a while, the merchant dismissed himself. Outside, he asked Timothy, "What is the secret of this man's power? I have never seen anything like it before!"

Timothy replied, "Paul is in love."

Puzzled, the merchant asked, "In love?"

"Yes," Timothy said. "Paul is in love with Jesus Christ."

Even more bewildered, the businessman asked, "Is that all?"

Timothy smiled. "That is *everything!*"

The Bible says, "We love because He first loved us" (1 John 4:19, NBV).

Second, Paul had divine appointments with Jews in Rome. "Three days later [Paul] called together the leaders of the Jews" (v. 17). Paul wasted no time to begin reaching out to unconverted Jews. He apparently had many divine appointments with his own Jewish people. One writer commented, "There were eleven large Jewish synagogues in Rome. The Christians in Rome had left these synagogues entirely alone. The Lord is now appointing Paul to convey the gospel to all these Roman Jews. This is precisely what Paul did immediately on reaching Rome. . . . For two years Paul pursued this task among the Jews in Rome. He converted at least four or five of the synagogues in Rome."[4]

Third, Paul had divine appointments with pagans in Rome. God had wonderfully led him and protected him en route to the capital city. Many people would meet Jesus Christ through Paul's ministry.

Paul witnessed to Roman soldiers. Chained to soldier after soldier on regular shifts, Paul exemplified Christ and testified for Christ. Though physically in chains, Paul was spiritually free—and effective! In one of his last letters, Paul wrote, "Now I want you to know, brothers, that what has happened to me has really served to advance the gospel. As a result, it has become clear throughout the whole palace guard and to everyone else that I am in chains for Christ. Because of my chains, most of the brothers in the Lord have been encouraged to speak the word of God more courageously and fearlessly" (Phil. 1:12-14). Guards had to be rotated frequently because of the rapid rate of their conversions. And those new baby Christians couldn't resist telling what had happened to them; it spread like wildfire through the Praetorian guard!

Paul witnessed to the household of Caesar. How and when Paul did so is not recorded, but he wrote from Rome to the Christians in Philippi: "All the saints send you greetings, especially those who belong to Caesar's household" (Phil. 4:22).

Paul witnessed to Nero Caesar Augustus. Though not recorded in the Bible, the fact of that meeting is based on the legal implications: "You have appealed to Caesar. To Caesar you will go!" (25:12). It is based on strong traditions, also. But most important, it is based on God's promise, "You must stand trial before Caesar" (27:24). And God is the Keeper of every promise!

Octavius had first adopted the title Augustus, meaning "most reverend." Caesar, the title for "emperor," became Czar in Russian and Kaiser in German—self-exalted titles.

When Paul came to Rome, Nero was Caesar. In his late 20s, Nero had already stained his sensual fingers with the bloody assassination of his own mother, Agrippina, and his wife, Octavia. His mistress and eventual second wife, Poppaea, was a Jewish proselyte—more evidence that ceremonies do not change the heart.

Nero had been born about the time of Paul's conversion on the Damascus Road. Having lived in the emperor's palace since age 17, Nero became emperor at age 24. Believing himself to be greater than any man who had ruled before him, Nero moved out of the Palace of the Caesars and built his Golden Palace, using the most elaborate materials then known to man. His new palace had its own high altar—a monument to himself.

Quickly exhausting the thrills of music and art, Nero turned to sexual orgies and soon degenerated into homosexuality. Unsatisfied with the monumental trophies of an emperor, Nero declared himself to be a living god. And there he sat in his spectacular palace, nearly a mile long and designed into a half-moon shape.

What a dramatic moment that divine appointment must have been! Ruth and I stood in that very spot, and I was filled with deep emotion. How I would like to have been there on that fateful day in the throne room of Domus Aurelia—the Palace of Gold.

That confrontation was one of contrasts. Nero, bored with life, every appetite satiated by abuse, living in constant fear for his life, sat on his golden throne so heavy it required a special foundation. His crown weighed heavy upon his head. Before him stood the little, skinny preacher, the apostle Paul. He was chained, but full of vigor and life. He had nothing to lose and everything to gain. What a message it must have been—telling Nero about Jesus Christ, who alone satisfies the longings of the heart, who came bringing life more abundantly. Paul's heart was brimful of joy, but not Nero's. Nero was emperor, but he couldn't go anywhere; people were plotting to kill him and take his empire from him. Nero was confined to his palace for safety. Paul was chained, but he could come and go, visiting freely with a long line of guests day after day.

Who was the real prisoner?

An old temple wall revealed the picture of a king forging a chain from his crown. Another picture portrayed a slave making a crown out of his chain. Beneath the pictures was inscribed: "Life is what one makes it, no matter of what it is made." We can, if we choose, make this world a palace or a prison!

Jesus Leads to an Unfinished Task (vv. 30-31)

"For two whole years Paul stayed there in his own rented house and welcomed all who came to see him. Boldly and without hindrance he preached the kingdom of God and taught about the Lord Jesus Christ" (vv. 30-31).

Paul may have been released for a time in which he is alleged to have traveled to Spain, Crete, and other Mediterranean spots. Either way, Paul ended up in the Mamertine prison. His prison became his pulpit. He taught those who came and wrote powerful letters to those who could not come—letters such as Ephesians, Philippians, Colossians, Philemon, and finally his very last, 2 Timothy. How much he enriched the church by these letters!

The Book of Acts leaves Paul in bonds for Jesus, but we leave him still at work for Jesus. Though he is bound, God's Word is not! The Philippian church sent contributions to help Paul in prison. He wrote back, "I am amply supplied, now that I have received from Epaphroditus the gifts you sent. They are a fragrant offering, an acceptable sacrifice, pleasing to God. And my God will meet all your needs according to his glorious riches in Christ Jesus" (Phil. 4:18-19).

The Book of Acts doesn't seem to have an ending. It just stops, like an Unfinished Symphony. There's no finale—not yet! The Book of Acts is still being written. It's an unfinished story—the era of the Holy Spirit at work through His people, the Church. Paul may end on the chopping block, but, like John the Baptist, "He himself was not the light; he came only as a witness to the light" (John 1:8). The Book of Acts is not the story of Paul; it is the story of the living Christ and the Holy Spirit working through God's people in the first century and showing the way for us in our day.

Paul's last recorded words from his prison cell ring with victory: "The time has come for my departure. I have fought the good fight, I have finished the race, I have kept the faith. Now there is in store for me the crown of righteousness, which the Lord, the righteous Judge, will award to me on that day—and not only to me, but also to all who have longed for his appearing. . . . The Lord . . . will bring me safely to his heavenly kingdom. To him be glory for ever and ever. Amen" (2 Tim. 4:6-8, 18).

While Paul's work concluded, God's unfinished task goes on in our day—as we pray, as we knock on lonely doors, as we minister to the sick, as we guide our families, as we grow in God's Word, as we introduce our circle of influence to Jesus, as we stand before classes and congregations, as we bond together in Christ's love.

Albert Schweitzer defined our unfinished task: "He comes to us, as of old, by the lakeside, He came to those who knew Him not. He speaks to us the same words, 'Follow Me' and sets us to the tasks which He has to fulfill for our time. He commands. And to those who obey Him, He will reveal Himself in the toils, the conflicts, the sufferings which they shall pass through in His fellowship. And, as an ineffable mystery, they shall learn in their own experience who He is."

Notes

Preface

1. Lloyd John Ogilvie, *The Communicator's Commentary,* vol. 5 (Waco, Tex.: Word Books, Publishers, 1983), 301.

Chapter 1

1. Charles Ludwig, "Paul's Success in Athens," *Herald of Holiness,* July 15, 1980, 11.
2. Ray C. Stedman, *Growth of the Body* (Santa Ana, Calif.: Vision House Publishers, 1976), 116.
3. Roy L. Smith, *Making a Go of Life* (New York: Abingdon Press, 1948), 269.
4. Edward J. O'Heron, *Biblical Companions* (Huntington, Ind.: Our Sunday Visitor, 1979), 159-60.
5. John Henry Jowett, *My Daily Meditation* (La Verne, Calif.: El Camino Press, 1975), 287.
6. Author unknown.
7. C. D. Hansen, "The Word Is Proclaimed," *Come Ye Apart,* June 19, 1976.

Chapter 2

1. Ludwig, *Herald of Holiness,* 10-11.
2. Bill Bright, *Revolution Now* (San Bernardino, Calif.: Campus Crusade for Christ, 1969), 89.

Chapter 3

1. An unidentifiable periodical source.
2. William M. Greathouse, *The Fullness of the Spirit* (Kansas City: Beacon Hill Press of Kansas City, n.d.), 28-29.
3. James S. Stewart, *Heralds of God* (New York: Charles Scribner's Sons, 1956), 129.
4. Stedman, *Growth of the Body,* 145-46.
5. Arnold E. Airhart, *Beacon Bible Expositions,* vol. 5, *Acts* (Kansas City: Beacon Hill Press of Kansas City, 1977), 218.
6. Greathouse, *Fullness of the Spirit,* 34.
7. Lloyd John Ogilvie, *Drumbeat of Love* (Waco, Tex.: Word Books, Publishers, 1976), 235.
8. Harold Ivan Smith, "Time for Advent," *Herald of Holiness,* n.d.

Chapter 4

1. William McCumber, "Sleeping in Church," *Herald of Holiness,* July 15, 1980, 18.

2. James S. Stewart, *King for Ever* (Nashville: Abingdon Press, 1975), 160.

Chapter 5

1. Norman Vincent Peale, *You Can Have God's Help with Daily Problems* (Pawling, N.Y.: Foundation for Christian Living, 1980), 34.

2. M. R. DeHaan, *Pentecost and After* (Grand Rapids: Zondervan Publishing House, 1964), 155.

3. Ibid., 160.

4. Howard LaFay, "Be Ye Men of Valour," *National Geographic* 128, no. 2 (August 1965): 169.

5. Henry Jacobsen, *The Acts Then and Now* (Wheaton, Ill.: Victor Books, 1973), 190.

6. Dwight L. Carlson, *Living God's Will* (Old Tappan, N.J.: Fleming H. Revell Co., 1976), 39.

7. *Nazarene Preacher,* May 1970.

Chapter 6

1. F. F. Bruce, *Commentary on the Book of the Acts,* in *The New International Commentary on the New Testament* (Grand Rapids: Wm. B. Eerdmans Publishing Co., 1976), 473.

2. Jacobsen, *Acts Then and Now,* 198.

3. William F. Kerr, ed., *Ministers' Research Service* (Wheaton, Ill.: Tyndale House Publishers, 1972), 33.

4. George W. Truett, *The Salt of the Earth* (Grand Rapids: Wm. B. Eerdmans Publishing Co., 1949), 151.

5. Harry Rich, *Come Ye Apart,* unidentified issue.

Chapter 7

1. DeHaan, *Pentecost and After,* 166.

2. William Owen Carter, *The Acts of the Apostles* (Nashville: Broadman Press, 1916), 250-51.

3. William P. Barker, *They Stood Boldly* (Westwood, N.J.: Fleming H. Revell Co., 1967), 172.

4. Jacobsen, *Acts Then and Now,* 205.

Chapter 8

1. William A. Tolbert, *Herald of Holiness,* August 1, 1978, 3. (Article unidentified)

2. George and Donna Rench, *Spice and Rice* (Kansas City: Beacon Hill Press of Kansas City, 1979), 55-58.

Chapter 9

1. William Graves, "Denmark, Field of the Danes," *National Geographic* 145, no. 2 (February 1974): 270.

2. John Oster, "Our Island of Need," *Christ for the Nations* (Kansas City: Nazarene Publishing House, 1978), 10.

3. Jacobsen, *Acts Then and Now,* 220.

4. R. C. H. Lenski, *The Interpretation of the Acts of the Apostles* (Minneapolis: Augsburg Publishing House, 1961), 941.

Bibliography

Airhart, Arnold E. *Beacon Bible Expositions.* Vol. 5, *Acts.* Kansas City: Beacon Hill Press of Kansas City, 1977.

Alford, Henry. *The New Testament for English Readers.* Chicago: Moody Press, n.d.

Banks, Louis Albert. *Paul and His Friends.* New York: Funk and Wagnalls Co., 1898.

Barclay, William. *God's Young Church.* Philadelphia: Westminster Press, 1970.

———. *The Acts of the Apostles; The Daily Study Bible.* Philadelphia: Westminster Press, 1953.

Barker, William P. *Saints in Aprons and Overalls.* Westwood, N.J.: Fleming H. Revell Co., 1959.

———. *They Stood Boldly.* Westwood, N.J.: Fleming H. Revell Co., 1967.

Benson, Joseph. *Benson's Commentary.* Vol. 4. New York: T. Mason and G. Lane, 1839.

Blaikie, William G. *A Manual of Bible History.* New York: Ronald Press Co., 1940.

Blair, Edward P. *The Acts and Apocalyptic Literature.* New York: Abingdon-Cokesbury Press, 1946.

Bright, Bill. *Revolution Now.* San Bernardino, Calif.: Campus Crusade for Christ, 1969.

Bruce, F. F. *Commentary on the Book of the Acts,* in *The New International Commentary on the New Testament.* Grand Rapids: Wm. B. Eerdmans Publishing Co., 1976.

———. *New Testament History.* Garden City, N.Y.: Doubleday and Co., 1971.

Buttrick, George Arthur, ed. *The Interpreter's Bible.* Vol. 9. New York: Abingdon Press, 1954.

Carlson, Dwight L. *Living God's Will.* Old Tappan, N.J.: Fleming H. Revell Co., 1976.

Carter, Charles W., and Earle, Ralph. *The Evangelical Commentary on the Acts of the Apostles.* Grand Rapids: Zondervan Publishing House, 1959.

Carver, William Owen. *The Acts of the Apostles.* Nashville: Broadman Press, 1916.

Clarke, Adam. *Clarke's Commentary.* Vol. 5. New York: Abingdon Press, n.d.

Davidson, F., ed. *The New Bible Commentary.* Grand Rapids: Wm. B. Eerdmans Publishing Co., 1958.

Davies, G. Henton; Richardson, Allen; and Wallis, Charles L., eds. *Twentieth Century Bible Commentary.* New York: Harper and Brothers, Publishers, 1955.

DeHaan, M. R. *Pentecost and After.* Grand Rapids: Zondervan Publishing House, 1964.

Demaray, Donald E. *The Book of Acts.* Grand Rapids: Baker Book House, 1959.

Ellicott, Charles John, ed. *A Bible Commentary for English Readers.* Vol. 7. London: Cassell and Co., n.d.

Fallis, William J. *Studies in Acts.* Nashville: Broadman Press, 1949.

Graves, William. "Denmark, Field of the Danes" *National Geographic* 145, no. 2 (February 1974).

Greathouse, William M. *The Fullness of the Spirit.* Kansas City: Nazarene Publishing House, 1958.

Halley, Henry H. *Bible Handbook.* Grand Rapids: Zondervan Publishing House, 1959.

Hansen, C. D. "The Word Is Proclaimed." *Come Ye Apart.* June 19, 1976.

Henry, Carl F. H., ed. *The Biblical Expositor.* Vol. 3. Philadelphia: A. J. Holman Co., 1960.

Henry, Matthew. *Matthew Henry's Commentary on the Whole Bible.* Edited by Leslie F. Church. Reprint. Grand Rapids: Zondervan Publishing House, 1961.

Hervey, A. C. "The Acts of the Apostles." In *The Pulpit Commentary.* Vol. 2. Edited by H. D. M. Spence and Joseph S. Excell. London: Funk and Wagnalls Co., 1908.

Jacobsen, Henry. *The Acts Then and Now.* Wheaton, Ill.: Victor Books, a division of SP Publications, 1973.

Jowett, John Henry. *My Daily Meditation.* La Verne, Calif.: El Camino Press, 1975.

Kerr, William F., ed. *Ministers' Research Service.* Wheaton, Ill.: Tyndale House Publishers, 1972.

Kingsley, Florence Morse. *Paul: A Herald of the Cross.* Philadelphia: Henry Altemus, 1890.

LaFay, Howard. "Be Ye Men of Valour." *National Geographic* 128, no. 2 (August 1965).

LaSor, William Sanford. *Church Alive.* Glendale, Calif.: Regal Books, a division of G/L Publications, 1972.

———. *Great Personalities of the New Testament.* Westwood, N.J.: Fleming H. Revell Co., 1961.

Lenski, R. C. H. *The Interpretation of the Acts of the Apostles.* Minneapolis: Augsburg Publishing House, 1961.
Ludwig, Charles. "Paul's Success in Athens." *Herald of Holiness.* July 15, 1980.
McCumber, William E. "Sleeping in Church." *Herald of Holiness.* July 15, 1980.
Mayfield, Joseph H., and Earle, Ralph. *Beacon Bible Commentary.* Vol. 7, *John; Acts.* Kansas City: Beacon Hill Press of Kansas City, 1965.
Morgan, G. Campbell. *The Acts of the Apostles.* Westwood, N.J.: Fleming H. Revell Co., 1924.
———. *An Exposition of the Whole Bible.* Westwood, N.J.: Fleming H. Revell Co., 1959.
Ogilvie, Lloyd John. *The Communicator's Commentary.* Vol. 5. Lloyd John Ogilvie, editor. Waco, Tex.: Word Books, Publishers, 1983.
———. *Drumbeat of Love.* Waco, Tex.: Word Books, Publishers, 1976.
O'Heron, Edward J. *Biblical Companions.* Huntington, Ind.: Our Sunday Visitor, 1979.
Oster, John. "Our Island of Need," *Christ for the Nations.* Kansas City: Nazarene Publishing House, February 1978.
Peale, Norman Vincent. *You Can Have God's Help with Daily Problems.* Pawling, N.Y.: Foundation for Christian Living, 1980.
Pfeiffer, Charles F. *Baker's Bible Atlas.* Grand Rapids: Baker Book House, 1961.
Pfeiffer, Charles F., and Harrison, Everett F., eds. *The Wycliffe Bible Commentary.* Chicago: Moody Press, 1962.
Rench, George and Donna. *Spice and Rice: The Story of the Church of the Nazarene in Indonesia.* Kansas City: Beacon Hill Press of Kansas City, 1979.
Robertson, Archibald Thomas. *Word Pictures in the New Testament.* Vol. 3. Nashville: Broadman Press, 1930.
Smith, Harold Ivan. "Time for Advent," *Herald of Holiness,* n.d.
Smith, Roy L. *Making a Go of Life.* New York: Abingdon Press, 1948.
Stedman, Ray C. *Growth of the Body.* Santa Ana, Calif.: Vision House Publishers, 1976.
Stewart, James S. *Heralds of God.* New York: Charles Scribner's Sons, 1956.
———. *King for Ever.* Nashville: Abingdon Press, 1975.

Stirling, John F. *An Atlas Illustration of the Apostles and the Epistles.* New York: Fleming H. Revell Co., n.d.

Taylor, Kenneth. *The Living Bible.* Wheaton, Ill.: Tyndale House Publishers, 1971.

Thomas, W. H. Griffith. *Outline Studies in the Acts of the Apostles.* Grand Rapids: Wm. B. Eerdmans Publishing Co., 1956.

Tolbert, William A. *Herald of Holiness,* August 1, 1978.

Truett, George W. *The Salt of the Earth.* Grand Rapids: Wm. B. Eerdmans Publishing Co., 1949.

Unger, Merrill F. *Unger's Bible Handbook.* Chicago: Moody Press, 1967.

Vaughn, Curtis. *Acts: A Study Guide.* Grand Rapids: Zondervan Publishing House, 1974.